The American Encounter with Islam

Introducing Islam

The American Encounter with Islam

Anjum Mir

To my family, but especially to my sons who send me soaring and keep me grounded all at once

Produced by OTTN Publishing, Stockton, New Jersey

Mason Crest Publishers
370 Reed Road
Broomall, PA 19008
www.masoncrest.com

3 5 7 9 8 6 4 2

Library of Congress Cataloging-in-Publication Data

Mir, Anjum.
  The American encounter with Islam / Anjum Mir.
      p. cm. — (Introducing Islam)
  Includes bibliographical references and index.
  Contents: What America Knows about Islam — The faith of Islam — A forgotten
  legacy : Muslim explorers and enslaved Africans — A growing faith :
  immigrants, converts, and Muslim communities — Islamic roots: the African-
  American encounter with Islam — American Muslim life : Islamic living —
  family, community, and American Muslim culture — Challenges facing Muslims
  in America.
  ISBN 1-59084-699-0
  1. Islam—United States—Juvenile literature. 2. Muslims—United States—
  Juvenile literature. 3. African Americans—Religion—Juvenile literature. [1.
  Islam. 2. Muslims.] I. Title. II. Series.
  BP67.U6M57 2004
  297'.0973—dc22
                              2003023819

Contents

Introduction

The central belief of Islam, one of the world's major religions, is contained in a simple but powerful phrase: "There is no god but Allah, and Muhammad is his prophet." The Islamic faith, which emerged from the Arabian desert in the seventh century C.E., has become one of the world's most important and influential religions.

Within a century after the death of the prophet Muhammad, Islam had spread throughout the Arabian Peninsula into Europe, Africa, and Asia. Today Islam is the world's fastest-growing religion and Muslims can be found throughout the globe. There are about 1.25 billion Muslims, which means that approximately one of every five people follows Islam. The global total of believers has surpassed two older religions, Hinduism and Buddhism; only Christianity has more followers.

Muslims can also be found in North America. Many Muslims have immigrated to the United States and Canada, and large numbers of people—particularly African Americans—have converted to Islam since the 1960s. Today, there are an estimated 6 million Muslims in the United States, with an additional half-million Muslims in Canada.

Despite this growing popularity, many people in the West are uninformed about Islam. For many Americans, their only exposure to this important religion, with its glorious history and rich culture, is through news reports about wars in Muslim countries, terrorist attacks, or fundamentalist denunciations of Western corruption.

The purpose of the INTRODUCING ISLAM series is to provide an objective examination of Islam and give an overview of what Muslims believe, how they practice their faith, and what values they hold most important. Four volumes in particular focus on Islamic beliefs and religious practices. *Islam: The Basics* answers the essential questions about the faith and provides information about the major sects. *Islam, Christianity, and Judaism* describes and explains the similarities and differences between these three great monotheistic religions. *Heroes and Holy Places* gives information about such important figures as Muhammad and Saladin, as well as shrines like Mecca and Jerusalem. *Islamic Fundamentalism* focuses on the emergence of the Islamist movement during the 20th century, the development of an Islamist government in Iran, and the differences between Islamists and moderates in such countries as Algeria, Indonesia, and Egypt.

Two volumes in the series explore Islam in the United States, and the relationship between the Muslim world and the West. *The American Encounter with Islam* provides specific history about Muslims in North America from the 17th century until the present, and traces the development of uniquely American sects like the Nation of Islam. *Muslims and the West* attempts to put the encounter between two important civilizations in broader perspective from a historical point of view.

Recent statistical data is extensively provided in two volumes, in order to discuss life in the Muslim world. *Who Are the Muslims?* is a geopolitical survey that explores the many different cultures that can be found in the Muslim world, as well as the different types of Islamic governments. *What Muslims Think and How They Live* uses information collected in a landmark survey of the Islamic world by the Gallup Organization, as well as other socioeconomic data, to examine Muslim attitudes toward a variety of questions and issues.

As we enter a new century, cultural and political tensions between Muslims and non-Muslims continue. Now more than ever, it is important for people to learn more about their neighbors of all faiths. It is only through education and tolerance that we will be able to build a new world in which fear and mistrust are replaced with brotherhood and peace.

Islam in America's heartland: Muslims in Cedar Rapids, Iowa, gather outside their mosque after Sunday prayers. The Muslim community in Cedar Rapids dates to the early 20th century.

What Americans Know About Islam

The last light of the setting sun washes over an expansive, domed hall dotted with people. Some sit, silent and cross-legged, beside the great pillars that sustain the ceiling; others are bowed down with their foreheads pressed against the ornate carpet; and still others chat softly and laugh together along the periphery and in the rear of the great room. Speaking in Arabic, a bearded man offers a casual greeting to a newcomer who removes his shoes at the entrance and deposits them in a cubby on the back wall. Dressed in an austere, floor-length robe and a scarf tightly wrapped around her head, a mother bearing an infant moves toward the back where a group of women has converged. She exchanges greetings and kisses with the others. Then, cradling her child in her arms, she faces forward, lips moving in silent prayer, and begins to bend and bow. The crowd, scattered about, produces a soft murmur, punctuated by the occasional cough or laugh, which echoes in the hall. Then, cutting the silence, a voice sounds over the loudspeaker in Arabic, and the haphazard crowd forms into neat rows—men in the front, women behind. At the head of the congregation, a man raises his hands to his shoulders, folds them across his chest, and begins a melodic Arabic recitation.

This scene, of a typical evening prayer at a *mosque*, could well be taking place in the Middle East. But it is not. In this case, the worshippers are in a quiet town in the American Midwest.

On September 11, 2001, Muslim communities throughout the United States were thrust into the public eye. Many Americans were alarmed to find out that so many Muslims, followers of the Islamic faith, lived within U.S. borders. The U.S. census does not collect data on religious affiliation, so it is difficult to say with precision how many Muslims there are in the United States. But recent estimates have put the number at about 6 million. Some of these people are immigrants, and some are American-born converts from other religions, but a growing number are born and raised as Muslims in the United States. The community is growing so fast that some experts predict Islam will soon surpass Judaism as the religion with the second-largest number of believers in the United States, after Christianity.

Despite the significant population of Muslims in the United States, many Americans know little about Islam. Many think that it represents a very different way of life. They are unaware that Islam has the same roots as Judaism and Christianity—that all three religions trace their origins to Abraham, that all three originated in the region currently referred to as the Middle East, and that all three consider Jerusalem to be a holy site. More important than common history, all three great religions share a similar system of values.

If many Jewish and Christian Americans don't know much

about Islam, many Muslims are themselves trying to figure out how they fit into American life. Should they blend in with "mainstream" society and risk losing their Islamic identity, or should they keep to themselves and perhaps be misunderstood by other Americans? What Muslims have discovered over the years is that neither blending in nor isolating themselves is an effective way to promote understanding—blending in makes Islam invisible and isolation makes it strange. Because of the diversity of backgrounds and approaches in the Muslim community, finding a middle ground has been challenging. However, over the last two decades, Muslims have made it a priority to develop a way of life that

As many Muslims in the United States have observed, there is no inherent contradiction between being a devout follower of Islam and being a patriotic American. This photo was taken in Dearborn, Michigan—where one in five residents is of Arab ancestry—about a month after the September 11, 2001, terrorist attacks.

allows them to wear their Islamic and American identities at the same time.

How Americans See Islam

For centuries, Western scholars have portrayed Islam and Muslims as mysterious, barbaric, inferior, and even evil. Attitudes such as these made it easier for Europeans to take over Muslim lands during the colonial period—and to justify colonialism as a means of bringing enlightenment and civilization to Muslims. European colonialism colored the relationship of Islam and the West, forever placing them at odds in the minds of Muslims and westerners alike.

As more Europeans settled in the United States, these Orientalist ideas came with them and became a part of the American world-view. Muhammad Alexander Russell Webb, who embraced Islam during his time as the U.S. consul in the Philippines, was the first known Anglo-American to convert to Islam. He spoke about the Western perception of Islam in 1893 at the World Parliament of Religions in Chicago.

> I am an American of the Americans. I carried with me for years the same errors that thousands of Americans carry with them today. Those errors have grown into history, false history has influenced your opinion of Islam. It influenced my opinion of Islam and when I began, ten years ago, to study the Oriental religions, I threw Islam aside as altogether too corrupt for consideration. But when I came beneath the surface, to know what Islam really is, to know who and what the prophet of Arabia was, I changed my belief very materially, and am proud to say that I am now a Mussulman [Muslim].

Upon seeing Muslims praying at the same event, a newspaper columnist wrote, "A lot a fellers was blacker than a pair o' shoes on Sunday morning. . . . You can't tell whether they're at prayer or a dog fight, but I suppose it's all the same in Arabia." His understanding that the followers of Islam were a non-white, Arabian community was common among Americans at the time and still exists today.

MUSLIMS AND VIOLENCE

Many Americans continue to see Islam as the "them" in an "us versus them" struggle. The notion that Islam is a "violent religion" and a threat to the United States has been especially prevalent since the terrorist attacks of September 11, 2001. The hijackers who crashed jetliners into the World Trade Center and Pentagon were members of an Islamic organization, al-Qaeda, which justified their actions by framing them as part of a *jihad* against the United States. Yet, as Muslim leaders and scholars quickly pointed out, the terrorist attacks actually violated Islamic teachings. The Qur'an, Islam's holy book, instructs Muslims to fight only if they are being unjustly oppressed or attacked, and, more important, Islamic tradition forbids Muslims to attack or injure civilians, women, and children.

Even the term *jihad* itself is widely misunderstood in the West. The word—which is often mistranslated in the mass media as "holy war," and used to denote violence perpetrated by Muslims in the name of their religion—simply means "effort" or "struggle." And in the sense most often used in the Qur'an, jihad actually refers to the inner struggle that each person makes to improve his or her character and spiritual state. Physical struggles that involve human violence have a separate term, *qital*.

ISLAM IN AMERICA

Positive or negative, there has definitely been a surge in interest about Islam and Muslims in recent years. While once there was a shortage of English-language material on Islam, now there are hundreds of books on the subject. Americans can go to any bookstore or library and find copies of the Qur'an as well as books with a variety of opinions on Islam. Though some promote negative views, many make an honest attempt to illuminate more about the people and the religion. Not only are Americans inquiring about the worldwide Islamic community, they are also more curious

These children attending a Sunday Arabic class in Cedar Rapids are among the estimated 6 million Muslims in the United States. Islam is the nation's fastest-growing religion.

about their own Muslim neighbors. What they are discovering is that Muslims are like everyone else—they are mothers and fathers, husbands and wives, sons and daughters. They may be doctors or lawyers, teachers or students, business managers or laborers. For recreation, they might go to a concert or a movie or a basketball game. And, like many Americans, they strive to make a positive difference in the lives of others.

For their part many American Muslims have concluded that, in light of recent events, they can no longer exist quietly. With their numbers growing, Muslims are finally venturing out. They are speaking out about their religion, participating in interfaith dialogues, and becoming more involved with American life.

American Muslims are a part of the *umma*, the larger world

community of Muslims. Clearly, however, they have their own distinct history and are developing a unique culture. No other Muslim population on the globe is as ethnically, racially, and ideologically diverse. Coming from many different countries, American Muslims have a variety of cultural practices, ideas, and identities. Yet, like colorful tiles of a mosaic picture, they are bonded together by a common belief in the basic tenets of the Islamic faith. At the same time, the Muslim community in the United States is constantly changing and evolving as new circumstances and challenges emerge.

The Kaaba, a shrine situated within Mecca's Masjid Al-Haram, or Great Mosque, is considered Islam's holiest site. Muslims believe the structure was originally created by Adam as a place to worship God, was destroyed in the Great Flood, and was later rebuilt by the patriarch Abraham and his son Ishmael.

The Islamic Faith

In order to understand the Muslim experience in America, it is crucial to understand the history and teachings of Islam as a whole. American Muslims, diverse in their cultures, races, and ethnicities, are united by their common Islamic heritage. They share the same basic beliefs and practices, and, like Muslims the whole world over, they trace the beginnings of their faith back about 1,400 years, to the western coastal region of Arabia, known as the Hejaz.

THE BIRTH OF ISLAM

Islam originated in Mecca, a city in the vast desert of present-day Saudi Arabia. Mecca was a flourishing market town located on the major trade routes between the Byzantine Levant (the eastern shores of the

Mediterranean), the Far East, and Africa. Merchants from all parts of Arabia traveled through Mecca, bringing business to the local population.

In addition to its commercial significance, Mecca had an important religious attraction—the *Kaaba*, an ancient temple that housed a collection of idols that symbolized the gods of the pagan Arabs. The Kaaba drew a constant stream of pilgrims who made the arduous desert journey to pay homage to the idols. So important was the Kaaba that each year the Arabs, who were often engaged in inter-tribal hostility and conflict, declared four months of peace so that pilgrims could have safe passage.

According to Islamic tradition, the Kaaba was originally built by Adam, was destroyed in the Great Flood, and was rebuilt by Abraham and his son Ishmael. Muslims consider both Adam and Abraham to be prophets, humans chosen by God to guide people to live a moral and just life under one God. Over time, a strong pagan culture prevailed over Arabia and filled the Kaaba with idols. Though some, mostly Christians and Jews, continued to recognize only one God, most worshipped the many idols representing various gods. It was into this environment, where the interchange of ideas was constant and where the notion of one God was a faint remnant of the past, that Muhammad was born in 570 C.E.

Muhammad was born into the distinguished tribe of the Quraysh. As guardians of the Kaaba, the Quraysh prospered from the business brought by the pilgrims who came to obtain blessings from the idols. At the age of six, Muhammad was orphaned with the death of his mother, Amina (his father, Abd Allah, had died months before Muhammad's birth). From then on, a series of relatives cared for and protected the boy. As was customary, Muhammad was sent to the country to live with a desert tribe so that he could learn refined language and manners. According to most Islamic sources, he never received a formal education and never learned to read or write.

As a youth, Muhammad's reliability and truthfulness earned

him the title "the Honest One." With a good reputation and a respected status in his tribe, he was able to pursue his interest in trade. When he was 25, a wealthy local businesswoman named Khadija hired him to manage a trade caravan to Syria. Captivated by his fairness, honesty, and kind character, the twice-widowed Khadija—who was 15 years Muhammad's senior—proposed marriage to him. He accepted. Khadija and Muhammad had six children: two sons, both of whom died in infancy, and four daughters.

Muhammad had never taken part in the idol worship of his tribe. Even as a child, he questioned the legitimacy of the idols of the Kaaba. While he was caring for his uncle's flocks in the hills of Mecca, he spent much of his time staring into the vast desert sky, contemplating a supreme being. The Arabs were not unfamiliar with this idea of one God, whom they knew in the past as *Allah*, an Arabic term signifying the Supreme God.

Throughout his adulthood, Muhammad retreated, with increasing regularity, from the busy life of Mecca to meditate in a secluded cave in the mountains just beyond his home. It was there in the year 610, at the age of 40, that he reportedly received his first revelation from God through the archangel Gabriel. "Read, in the name of your Lord who created man from a clot of blood." These first words Muhammad received from God are a part of the 96th chapter of the Qur'an.

When Muhammad began openly preaching his message, most Meccans reacted with disdain and doubt. And as the number of Muslims, or followers of Islam, grew, so too did the bitterness and hostility toward them. Fearing persecution, many new Muslims did not publicly practice their faith. Those who did risked losing their wealth, their businesses, and their homes; some even paid with their lives. At one point, the new Muslims were exiled from Mecca and forced to live in the hills, where they suffered starvation and illness. The persecution of the Muslims was so serious that on two occasions Muhammad asked a Christian king in Abyssinia (in modern-day Ethiopia) to provide asylum for his people. The king, struck by Islam's similarity to his own religion, offered the Muslims shelter and protection.

INTERSECTION BETWEEN ISLAM, CHRISTIANITY, AND JUDAISM

Early on, the Christian king of Abyssinia identified a kinship between his faith and Islam. Christianity and Islam—and Judaism as well—trace their origins to the patriarch Abraham. Jesus, the central figure in Christianity, came from the line of Isaac,

An angel stays the hand of Abraham, pointing to a ram God has provided for sacrifice in place of Abraham's son. The story of Abraham's sacrifice is among the traditions common to Judaism, Christianity, and Islam, the world's three major monotheistic faiths.

Abraham's younger son (as did the important Jewish prophet Moses, who led the Jews from captivity in Egypt); Muhammad and the Arabs are descendants of Ishmael, Abraham's first son.

According to the Qur'an, Islam is a continuation of the messages brought by the prophets of Judaism and Christianity. In fact, Jews and Christians, who also received scriptures (the Torah and the Bible), are called "People of the Book" and are accorded special status by Islam. The Qur'an is filled with accounts of Moses and Jesus, both of whom are considered key figures, are highly respected, and are a source of learning and inspiration for Muslims.

In addition to their common roots and prophets, Islam, Christianity, and Judaism share a common message: a belief in one supreme God and an emphasis on living a moral life. Whether in their private lives or in interactions with others, all three religious traditions emphasize their adherents' responsibility to practice honesty, sincerity, generosity, mercy, kindness, and justice.

THE EARLY ISLAMIC COMMUNITY

Social and economic injustice permeated the society in which Muhammad first began preaching the message of Islam. Meccan society was known for its bad treatment of the poor, orphans, women, and slaves. The wealthy and the leaders hoarded resources, were corrupt, and oppressed the lower classes. The Meccan leadership was particularly threatened by the growing Muslim community and the social and moral changes that it promoted—changes that would challenge their lavish lifestyles and the tribal traditions that secured their leadership. They were determined to stop Muhammad—or, at the very least, to make him and his followers endure a life of suffering. Relief came for the Muslims in 622, when the people of Yathrib, a city 200 miles north of Mecca, invited Muhammad and his followers to live in their city. They were impressed by reports of Muhammad's character and thought that, as a leader, he could cultivate peace between their quarrelsome tribes. The migration of Muslims to

Yathrib is known as the *hijra*. The people of Yathrib embraced Muhammad as their prophet and renamed their city Madinat al-Nabi, or "City of the Prophet." Later, the name would be shortened to Al-Madina; in the West, the inland city is known as Medina.

The move to Medina was a defining moment in Islamic history—it was the point at which Islam began to spread beyond its roots in Mecca. Under the skillful leadership of Muhammad, the small Muslim community of Medina established itself as an exem-

Medina, in present-day Saudi Arabia, is Islam's second-holiest city. It was here that Muhammad and his followers settled after being forced from Mecca in 622. In the foreground of this photo is the Holy Mosque of the Prophet.

plary society. Muhammad was able to break tribal barriers and establish laws and a form of leadership that was previously unheard of in Arabia. He even established a set of individual peace agreements with various political communities of Medina. This collection of agreements, which sought to regulate the relations between the Muslim community and its neighboring Jewish tribes, was called the Constitution of Medina.

During Muhammad's lifetime, the Islamic state that started in Medina grew into an empire that included most of Arabia. Many modern-day Muslims fondly refer to this period as the "golden age" of Islam—a time when the Prophet himself was available to Muslims and, with God's guidance, could explain the divine messages. When new questions about religion arose in the community, he would receive a revelation with an answer. After Muhammad's death, Muslims have had to rely on the Qur'an, Muhammad's example, and their own intellect to answer questions about their faith and practice.

THE QUR'AN, THE SUNNA, AND ISLAMIC LAW

Beginning in Mecca in 610 and throughout the remainder of his life, Muhammad intermittently received the Qur'an through the angel Gabriel. The revealed verses focused on a range of issues. Often they addressed specific social concerns of the growing Muslim community. Upon receiving revelations, Muhammad shared them with his people. The revelations were preserved in various forms during Muhammad's lifetime; an authoritative version of the Qu'ran was compiled years after the Prophet's death, during the reign of the third Muslim caliph, Uthman. The Qur'an was revealed in a language that impressed the poetry-loving people of Arabia.

Though portions of the holy book are easy to understand, even the most skilled scholars throughout history have struggled to grasp its deeper meanings. As a result, an entire science in Islamic history is devoted to studying and explaining the verses and meaning of the Qur'an. Nowadays, translations of the Qur'an and its explanations are available in many languages, including Swahili, Chinese, Spanish, and English. However, Most Muslims agree that the distinctive Arabic of the Qur'an cannot be accurately translated, so Muslims in the United States and all over the world still read and recite it in its original Arabic. Special honor is given to Muslims who memorize the entirety of the Qur'an—a task that is considered extraordinary now but was commonplace in early Islamic history. Several schools devoted to Qur'anic mastery have been established in the United States. In these schools, students also learn the beautiful art of recitation. Few sounds are more moving and inspiring than the high and low vibrato of a Qur'anic vocalist.

In addition to the Qur'an, the early Muslims carefully chronicled the details of Muhammad's life. They documented observations and reports of what he said and how he acted in a variety of private and public situations. The word *Sunna* ("custom") is used to refer to the totality of the Prophet's actions, sayings, and general way of being. Narration of the Sunna is known as *Hadith* ("traditions"). While Muslims use the Qur'an as their main source of guidance, they rely on the recorded traditions of the Prophet to fill in the details. For example, the Qur'an constantly commands people to pray, but it provides little instruction on how to pray. It is through the example and practice of Muhammad that Muslims learned the formal structure of prayer.

The message of the Qur'an is universal. It was meant for people living in all ages and not just in the time of Muhammad. Most scholars agree that it contains a general structure for religious laws and practice that applies wherever and whenever people live. For example, although the Qur'an says that people should generally dress in a modest way that doesn't show off their body, it doesn't tell people how exactly to dress because fashions and clothing change with time. The religious law that is extracted primarily from the Qur'an and Sunna is called the *Sharia*, which means "the way to God." Muslims look to the Sharia for rules regarding day-to-day life, including direction on worship, diet, family, finances, and human relations. There are special scholars who are trained to provide answers to questions about Islamic law.

THE MUSLIM COMMUNITY AFTER MUHAMMAD

After Muhammad's death in 632, the question arose as to who should succeed the Prophet as leader of the Islamic community. Most Muslims favored Abu Bakr, a longtime friend and confidant of Muhammad's said to be among the first converts to Islam. A small group, however, believed that Ali, Muhammad's cousin and son-in-law, should be the Prophet's successor because of their blood relationship. The majority, who prevailed in selecting Abu Bakr as Islam's first caliph, became known as the *Sunnis*, while the supporters of Ali became known as the *Shia* (or Shiites). Over the centuries, theological differences between these two groups emerged. Today the Sunnis and the Shiites, Islam's two major sects, coexist harmoniously in some areas but have had troubled relations in others.

Though Islam began in Arabia, it was never just an Arab religion, and within a century of Muhammad's death a vast Islamic empire—stretching from India through North Africa and into Europe's Iberian Peninsula—contained a mosaic of races and cultures. Islam spread into many areas through peaceful means, such as trade and commerce. In other regions, however, Islam was spread by the sword. Nonetheless, Muslim rulers were noteworthy for their generally tolerant attitudes toward non-Muslim subjects.

Another hallmark of the Islamic world was its emphasis on learning: while Europe muddled through the Middle Ages, the great cities of the Islamic world shone as centers of scholarship. Muslims founded the first universities and rose to the forefront of many fields, including fine arts, architecture, literature, philosophy, law, theology, natural sciences, medicine, mathematics, astronomy, and geography.

Over the years, however, the Islamic world fragmented, with rival caliphates ruling different regions, and empires rising and falling. The Ottoman Empire, based in modern-day Turkey, was the last great Islamic empire. Founded in the 14th century, the empire at one time included much of the present-day Middle East, North Africa, and southeastern Europe; after a long decline, it was finally dissolved completely by European colonial powers after World War I.

Today, though no Islamic empire exists any longer, Islam is the fastest-growing religion in the world, with about 1.25 billion followers. Islam is a major religion in Central Asia, in many parts of Africa, and even in eastern European countries such as Bosnia and Macedonia. There are an estimated 6 million to 8 million Muslims in the United States and another half-million in Canada, and significant Muslim communities can be found in some countries of South America.

THE TEACHINGS AND PRACTICE OF ISLAM

Many people are attracted to Islam for its combination of structural simplicity and spiritual depth. According to Islamic tradition, every human being is born close to God in a beautiful, pure state. Throughout life, the influences of the world, the necessities of everyday life, and the peculiarities of human nature cloud this once-ideal condition. The Qur'an invites people to constantly improve themselves and to attempt to regain the purity, beauty, and intimacy with God that are a part of their original nature. In this quest for beauty, Muslims are encouraged toward three levels of spiritual attainment: *islam* (submission), *iman* (faith), and *ihsan* (performance of good deeds).

Many theologians throughout Islamic history have observed that because Islam has various levels of spirituality, it appeals to a great diversity of people. As one American Muslim scholar eloquently explains: "The teachings of Islam have levels of meaning, and the religion consists of a hierarchy that, destined to become the religion of a large portion of humanity, had to accommodate the spiritual and intellectual needs of the simplest peasant and the most astute philosopher, the warrior and the lover, the jurist and the mystic."

Whereas a philosopher or a jurist might aspire toward a deeper understanding, a simple peasant may live his life in happiness at the most basic level of belief. For those who are motivated toward the highest levels of piety, the process is similar to that of learning—hard work and study lead to understanding, and understanding exercised with grace and discernment leads to wisdom. The transformation begins on the outside and moves inward.

ISLAM: THE SUBMISSION

Although the religion revealed to Muhammad has become known as Islam, this is also the name of the first stages of religious awareness. Focused on outward action, individuals at this level practice the basic requirements of the religion, morally, intellectually, and physically. Much of this first level is characterized by physical and social rituals. A committed Muslim undertakes these rituals and hopes that by being consistent and steadfast with these actions, he or she will move to the next level.

The word *Islam* comes from the Arabic word *aslama*, which means "surrendered"—in this case, to the will of Allah. The Islamic religion is built on this initial act of submission. The main elements of this commitment are the five foundational actions of Islam, commonly called the five pillars: *shahada*, a declaration of faith; *salat*, prayer five times daily; *zakat*, the giving of alms; *sawm*, fasting during the month of Ramadan; and *hajj*, the pilgrimage to Mecca. Each of these five actions emphasizes the idea that in order to gain true, internal belief, a person must first transform his or her actions to reflect a commitment to a closer relationship with God.

Five times a day, throughout Muslim lands, city and countryside alike reverberate with the **adhan,** or call to prayer. Be it the bustling marketplace of Cairo or the placid meadows of Turkey, the rousing refrains drift through the air and remind people to worship:

> God is most great. (four times)
> I bear witness that there is no god but God.
> I bear witness that Muhammad is the messenger of God.
> Hurry to the prayer.
> Hurry to salvation.
> God is most great.
> God is most great.
> There is no god but God.

In the call for *fajr* prayer, the dawn prayer, a verse is added that says: *Prayer is better than sleep.*

Echoed within the *adhan* is the first pillar of Islam—the *shahada,* or testimony of faith: "There is no god but God and Muhammad is God's messenger." The *shahada* is a verbal profession of God's unity and Muhammad's role as messenger. Because it defines the purpose of the remaining pillars, it is the initial act of Muslim life. Muslims learn the *shahada* at a very young age and then repeatedly recite it in their prayers throughout their lives. For those not born Muslims, the *shahada* is also the means to conversion: to become Muslim, all a person must do is recite it with conviction. Each year, through this simple act, many people join the growing population of Muslims in the United States.

The prophet Muhammad reportedly said that the second pillar, *salat,* or prayer, is the central and most basic act of a Muslim. Five times each day, Muslims are required to put aside their mundane activities and perform ritual prayers that consist not only of words, but also of physical actions—a series of postures and prostrations. Prayer times are spaced throughout the day: *fajr,* the early-morning prayer, comes before sunrise and often requires a person to wake from his or her sleep; *zuhr* and *asr*, the noon and late-afternoon prayers, are offered in the middle of busy workdays; *maghrib*, the evening prayer, is offered just after sunset; and *isha'*, the night prayer, falls after darkness. Before they pray, Muslims perform ablutions—ritual cleansing, called **wudu'**, that

Salat is one of the five pillars of Islam, the basic requirements of the faith. During the prayers, performed five times daily, Muslims all over the world face in the direction of Mecca.

demonstrates a readiness for worship. No matter where in the world they live, even in the United States, Muslims pray facing the direction of the Kaaba in Mecca. Described in the Qur'an as a symbolic house of God, the Kaaba unifies praying Muslims the world over. Because it requires discipline and consistency, most Muslims would agree that prayer is the most challenging of the five pillars.

Though individual worship is most common, Muslims can also pray in a group. Congregational prayers are lead by an *imam*. Many traditions of the Prophet place great value on the social aspect of worship. To emphasize this point, Muslim men are required to attend one group prayer during the week. According to some interpretations, it is recommended that Muslim women do so as well. Muslims congregate for *Juma* (Friday) prayer in the afternoon, typically at the peak of the workday. The *Juma* prayer takes the place of the *zuhr* prayer, one of the five daily prayers. Unlike Jews and Christians, who are supposed to rest from work on their Sabbath day, Muslims are not required to rest from work on Friday. However, in many Islamic countries, businesses and institutions are closed on Friday, so many Muslims do rest from work on that day. In countries where Friday is not a holiday, Muslims close their businesses and institutions during the congregational prayer and reopen when it is over. However, Muslim minorities in non-Islamic countries such as the United States often find it difficult to meet their prayer requirements in the workplace. Those Muslims who wish to fulfill their prayer obligations often attend prayer during their lunch hour or request special time off. Muslims who work in companies or business localities that have a significant number of Muslims often organize smaller group prayers in or near their workplaces. Young Muslims in colleges and universities organize campus prayers and often try to schedule their classes so that they don't conflict with Friday prayer. Many Muslim professionals and students even have requested special rooms in their businesses and schools where they can perform their daily prayers. Those who are still unable to perform their prayers on time have the option of making them up as soon as they are able.

Goodness and mercy are the two most frequently mentioned characteristics of God in the Qur'an. All but 2 of the 114 chapters of the holy book begin with the words, "In the Name of God, most Gracious, most Merciful." It is no wonder that Muslims are strongly encouraged to embrace these traits for themselves. The third pillar, *zakat* (alms tax), presents Muslims with the chance to put both of these qualities to work on a social level. Muslims are required to give a small percentage of their annual income to individuals or institutions in need of assistance. Though *zakat* is most often given to the poor, it can also be used to support students of religion, travelers, and those in debt. In addition to its social benefit, *zakat* is of vital importance to the individual giving it. The meaning of the word *zakat* is related to the Arabic term for "purity"; this pillar has thus been explained as a ritual that purifies a person's soul.

One month out of each year, Muslims observe the fourth pillar of Islam—*sawm*, or fasting during the holy month of Ramadan. From dawn until sunset Muslims above the age of adolescence abstain from all forms of food, drink, and sexual activity. Certain categories of people are excused from fasting; these include nursing mothers, menstruating and pregnant women, the elderly, and individuals with serious and chronic illnesses. If they are able, they can fulfill their obligations at a later time. A successful fast is one during which an individual also refrains from undesirable behavior such as gossiping, being dishonest, arguing, displaying anger, and wasting time. Muslims are encouraged to be especially aware of the needs of the poor and to spend their days serving the community, engaging in honest activities. Because Ramadan is the month during which Muhammad received the first Qur'anic revelation on a night called Laylat al-Qadr, "the Night of Power," Muslims often spend the month studying and reciting the Qur'an. Many individuals also take part in special night prayer called *Tarawih*, offered after the last of the five daily prayers. Through the course of the month, the entirety of the Qur'an is usually recited during these prayers. American Muslims frequently take the opportunity of Ramadan to celebrate breaking their fast in the evening and saying the night prayers with family and friends.

The true diversity of the Islamic world is most evident during the hajj, the fifth and final pillar of Islam. In recent years about 2 million Muslims have congregated annually in the city of Mecca, birthplace of Muhammad and site of the Kaaba. The pilgrimage draws Muslims from across the globe, including China, Europe, and North and South America. A rite originally established by Abraham, the hajj was adopted and expanded by Islam during the final year of Muhammad's life. The pilgrimage consists of a series of rituals, acts, and prayers. During the main ritual, Muslims circumambulate, or walk around, the Kaaba while reciting prayers and praises to God. On his transformative 1964 visit to Mecca, Malcolm X said, "There were tens of thousands of pilgrims, from all over the world. They were of all colors, from blue-eyed blondes to black-skinned Africans. But we were all participating in the same ritual, displaying a spirit of unity and brotherhood that my experiences in America had led me to believe never could exist between the white and non-white." If they are physically and financially able to make the journey, all Muslims are required to perform the hajj once in a lifetime.

IMAN: FAITH AND UNDERSTANDING

Pious Muslims observe the five required pillars of Islam throughout their lives. Inner faith, *iman*, is viewed as a gift from God to those who work the hardest at pleasing God by perfecting their actions and character. Muhammad described *iman* as "a knowledge in the heart, a voicing of the tongue, and an activity with the limbs." The faith consists of six central elements to which Muslims must adhere: belief in God's oneness, in angels, in revealed books, in prophets, in the Day of Judgment, and in *al-*

qadar (divine predestination).

As is evident from the *shahada*, the most important aspect of faith is belief in one God. Muslims believe that human beings are born knowing that there is only one God—one who is all-knowing, all-seeing, and always present everywhere. The belief in God's oneness is called **Tawhid**. The gravest sin, according to Islam, is associating partners with God—a sin referred to as *shirk* (that is, making anything equal to God or more important than Him). Because God is unique, He cannot be described as having a gender or physical characteristics as do human beings. In the Qur'an, God describes Himself as the absolute perfection of all

The annual hajj draws approximately 2 million Muslim pilgrims to Mecca. During the main ritual, the faithful walk around the Kaaba (seen at the center of this photo) seven times while reciting prayers and praises to God.

good and powerful qualities. God has ninety-nine names that represent this perfection—names such as the "All-Merciful," the "Infinitely-Good," the "Most Wise," the "Ultimate Artist," the "Most Beautiful," the "Truth," the "Most Just." Muslims and Arabic-speaking Jews and Christians throughout the world refer to this one common God as Allah, a generic Arabic term for "God." In Muslim understanding, God is part of the world that is beyond human perception—the unseen world. However, humans can see signs of His oneness, power, existence, and mercy in nature and creation.

As a part of faith, Muslims must also believe in the angels of God. In the Qur'an, angels play an important role. Like Gabriel, the angel that brought revelations to Muhammad, Moses, and Jesus, other angels also have specific tasks. The Qur'an describes these otherworldly beings as made of light and inherently good-natured. At the end of each prayer, Muslims greet two guardian angels, one on their left and one on their right, who are said to record the deeds of each individual. However, for the most part, these beings do not influence the everyday life of Muslims.

Belief in God's prophets and His revelation are two aspects of faith that go hand in hand in Islamic thought. God sent prophets to all people and nations. When God put humans on earth, Islam teaches, He also gave them guidance. So Adam, the first human, was also the first prophet. Muhammad is considered the final prophet. Accordingly, he is called "the seal of the prophets." Prophets are described as ordinary humans with extraordinary character who were chosen by God to guide humans or bring the message of God to humanity. Some prophets, such as Moses, Jesus, and Muhammad, had the added responsibility of bringing books of revelation. Believing in these books is a significant aspect of the Muslim faith. Muslims must accept not only the Qur'an, but also the Torah, which is the scripture of Jews, and the Bible, which is the scripture of Christians. Each is thought of as the word of God. In them, God gives guidance in language that humans can understand. For further guidance, Muslims believe, God sent prophets—role models who personify the principles of the holy books.

The Qur'an also mentions an end to time, when each individual will be held accountable for his or her actions—good and bad. Consequently, Muslims are encouraged to spend their time in this world doing good works, struggling to correct their character flaws, and improving their relationship with God. Paired with the belief in a final accounting is a belief in life after death. The Qur'an presents many images of reward for good deeds and punishment for evil ones in the afterlife. However, it is clear that the reward for the pious who draw close to God in this life will be nearness to Him in the next.

The final central element of the Islamic faith is belief that God determines everything and is in control of the universe.

IHSAN: TRUE BEAUTY

The deepest level of Islamic faith is *ihsan*. This stage of faith combines the outward acts of worship (such as the five pillars) with inner acts of worship. Individuals who reach this level are constantly aware of God. The Qur'an describes the actions of these people as beautiful and pure. Reflecting their inner beauty, they act with sincere kindness, mercy, and goodness. At this stage, according to Islamic teaching, a person's thoughts and feelings are in harmony with the person's actions. Above all, people who have achieved *ihsan* are close to God.

Sufism is the tradition practiced by many Muslims that is most focused on *ihsan*. In contrast to Sharia, or Islamic law, which focuses on a way to God through outward actions, Sufism focuses on an inner way to God through smaller prayers called *du'a* and through **dhikr**, remembrance of God. Sufism has become increasingly popular among American Muslims over the last few years.

Slaves in South Carolina, 1862. An estimated 7 to 10 percent of the West Africans brought to the New World in the transatlantic slave trade were Muslims, but Islam had largely died out among black Americans by the end of the Civil War.

Muslims During the Era of Slavery

Between the 16th and 19th centuries, an estimated 10 million black Africans were brought against their will to the Western Hemisphere, where they were sold as slaves. Some 600,000 to 650,000 ended up in the British North American colonies.

It is estimated that 7 to 10 percent of the slaves transported across the Atlantic Ocean were Muslims. Thus, Islam may have been introduced in America by as many as 65,000 enslaved West Africans. Nevertheless, most historians agree that the Islam brought by these West African natives had little long-term impact in the United States.

Until recently, very little scholarly attention was paid

to Islam in the United States during the antebellum (pre–Civil War) period. It was widely assumed that, after living for a period in Christian America, enslaved Africans abandoned the Islamic religion. However, ongoing research has shown that many African Muslims—mistakenly called Mohametans (Muhammadans) at the time—continued to profess and practice their faith. Even when they were compelled by their owners to publicly convert to

WELL-KNOWN ENSLAVED AFRICAN MUSLIMS

Job Ben Solomon Jallo

Islam, education, and an exceptional character were Job Ben Solomon Jallo's key to freedom. His story, unlike that of most slaves, is filled with good fortune. He was born Ayuba Suleiman Ibrahim Diallo around 1700. Originally from the Flube tribe in what is now Senegal, he came from a family of religious scholars and leaders. He was well versed in Arabic and the Qur'an.

In 1730, while on his way to sell two of his own family's slaves, Jallo was captured by a rival tribe and himself sold into slavery. He survived the difficult passage across the Atlantic aboard a slave ship and was sold to a Maryland planter. Jallo continued to maintain his Islamic identity and to practice his faith. After an escape in 1731, he was caught in Pennsylvania and imprisoned. Thomas Bluett, a minister who later wrote Jallo's biography, was impressed by his manner, civility, and devotion to his faith and obtained his release.

Jallo was sent to England in 1733. En route, he learned to speak and write English and impressed everyone when he transcribed the Qur'an from memory. In England, he met the royal family and did some translation for the British Museum. He later returned home to Africa and remained there until his death in 1773.

Abd al-Rahman Ibrahima

Ibrahima, a well-educated prince and military leader, was taken into bondage in 1788. For 15 years he was enslaved on a cotton and tobacco plantation in Natchez, Mississippi. After many failed escape attempts, he married a slave named Isabella. Together they had nine children.

An Arabic letter that Ibrahima wrote for a Natchez newspaper eventually reached the king of Morocco. Upon seeing the letter, which was clearly written by a fellow Muslim, the king requested Ibrahima's release. That request was granted in 1828.

But Ibrahima did not want to leave without his wife. Hearing of his plight, the community quickly raised enough money to buy her freedom. The couple traveled north, and Ibrahima embarked

Christianity, many Muslims continued to secretly practice Islam. Not only did this religious devotion give them a sense of dignity and inner strength, it connected them to their roots—it was one part of their African past that slave owners could not subdue.

Literacy was another great source of strength and identity for enslaved Muslims. Accounts of West Africa at the time reveal that Muslims were encouraged to learn Arabic and study the Qur'an.

on a speaking tour during which he explained his background, his religion, and his history. His character and knowledge impressed many white listeners, even those who did not favor the emancipation of slaves, and Ibrahima raised enough money to buy his children's freedom.

He returned to Africa in 1829. But the man who had been a prince when captured and sold into slavery more than 40 years earlier never made it back to his kingdom. Six months after his ship landed on the continent of his birth, he died of illness.

Omar ibn Said

"I was a teacher twenty-five years. There came a great army to my country. They killed many people. They took me to sea, and sold me to the hands of the Christians, who bound me, and sent me on board of a great ship." So begins Omar ibn Said's account of how he was taken from West Africa to be a slave in the United States.

Said, an Arabic scholar and teacher, arrived in Charleston, South Carolina, in 1807. After running away from his first master, he was captured in North Carolina and sold to a plantation owner there. He had the relative good fortune to be made a house slave, so his work was physically much easier than that of a field slave.

Though he claimed to have converted to Christianity, much evidence suggests that Said remained loyal to his Islamic heritage. When he copied the Bible in Arabic, he incorporated Qur'anic verses and the name of the prophet Muhammad. "The Lord's Prayer," the last manuscript that he wrote, actually paraphrased a chapter of the Qur'an.

Said left behind at least 14 Arabic manuscripts, among which is a 16-page Arabic autobiography. Historians both Muslim and Christian continue to research the life of this extraordinary man.

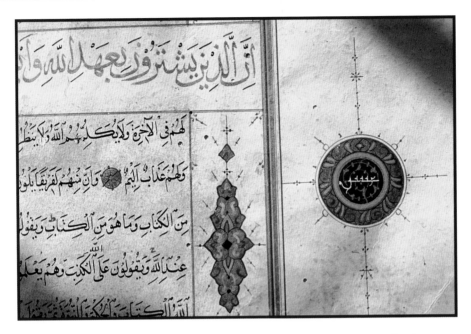

A page from the Qur'an. As a consequence of their religion's emphasis on study of the holy text, some West African Muslims taken into bondage were literate—a fact that challenged American slaveholders' notions about the inferiority of African peoples and cultures.

Lamine Kaba, a slave from a family of religious leaders, speaks of African Muslim literacy in his writings. He reveals that in addition to prominent men, peasants and women were also encouraged to be literate and educated in religion. He goes on to mention that some women surpassed men in learning and memorizing the Qur'an. The enslaved Muslims left a legacy of letters containing Qur'anic verses written by them in Arabic script. In addition to writing down the Qur'an from memory, some Muslim slaves actually acquired copies of the holy book. Surprisingly, copies of the Qur'an were often given to Muslim slaves by Christians who were sensitive to these slaves' religious commitment. In order to teach the Qur'an and Arabic, some slaves started small schools in a few communities.

Clearly, being literate was an advantage that Muslim slaves valued. For one thing, literacy gave them greater influence within the slave communities. (Of course, slave owners were in many cases harsher on literate slaves because they tended to be more confident and rebellious.) Some Muslims also earned their freedom because they could read and write. American and British philanthropists who were intrigued by well-educated slaves with strong Muslim identities bought them their freedom and sometimes helped them return to Africa; several also wrote biographies of Muslim slaves.

ISLAMIC IDENTITY AND PRACTICE

Prayer rugs and rosary beads left behind by enslaved Muslims reveal their devotion to the basic beliefs and practices of Islam. Most of the time, not surprisingly, Muslim slaves prayed in secret. But there were some exceptions. For example, Yarrow Mamout practiced his Islamic faith openly during his many years as a slave, from before the American Revolution to 1807, when he was freed. He remained a devout Muslim until his death, perhaps in 1844. By that time Mamout had become a successful businessman and prominent resident of Georgetown. In 1819, when the famous artist Charles Willson Peale painted his portrait, Mamout may already have been 103 years old—and he would live for another 25 years!

On Sapelo Island, off the coast of Georgia, there is further evidence that some enslaved Africans maintained their Muslim religious identity. When interviewed in the 1930s for an oral history project, descendants of a large slave community on the island still remembered their Muslim relatives. They spoke of the men wearing skullcaps and turbans and the women wearing veils. They also recalled vague details of Muslims praying, fasting during the month of Ramadan, and giving alms.

As on Sapelo Island, however, Islam originating in West Africa disappeared from the United States with the abolition of slavery and the passing of the former slaves. However, scholars continue to explore the legacy of Islamic culture and practice that the African Muslims left behind.

Arabs made up the first major wave of
Muslim immigrants to the United States,
during the last quarter of the 19th century.
While Arabs continue to come to U.S.
shores in significant numbers, today
Muslim immigrants hail from virtually all
parts of the Islamic world.

Immigrants, Converts, and Communities

Not long after the Civil War, Muslim immigrants—
who, unlike West African slaves, came to the
United States willingly—began making the journey from their homelands to American shores.
Muslims looked to start new lives in the United States
(and continue to do so) for the same reasons as other
immigrant groups. Some sought economic opportunity
or wished to further their education; others joined relatives who had immigrated earlier; and still others
came to escape grave conditions in their homeland.
Above all, many were drawn to the United States by
the promise of freedom.

Many early Muslim immigrants who came to the
United States for economic reasons were young men

43

who planned to work, save money, and then return to their homeland wealthy enough to live there comfortably. This goal has been called "the myth of return" because very few immigrants ever went back to their homeland. Lacking education or job skills—and, in some cases, hampered by social discrimination—many were only able to find low-paying work, and hence they never saved enough money to go back home. Others married, had children, and established roots in the community, which overrode plans to return to the country of their birth.

MUSLIM IMMIGRANTS TO THE UNITED STATES

The first identifiable wave of Muslim immigrants to the United States arrived between 1875 and 1912. They were mostly Syrian, Lebanese, and Palestinian Arabs living under Ottoman rule, and they followed an earlier wave of Arab Christian immigrants from the deteriorating Ottoman Empire. Not much is recorded about these early Muslim immigrants. Most were young, uneducated men who found jobs as peddlers or factory workers.

Many of the early Arab immigrants, both Christians and Muslims, settled in Detroit, Chicago, and other industrial cities of the Midwest. Here small Muslim communities had developed by the second decade of the 20th century. These Arab Muslims were soon joined by small numbers of Muslims from India, who had suffered discrimination under British colonial rule. Muslims from eastern Europe also made the ocean crossing to the United States. In fact, it was a group of Albanian immigrants that founded the first mosque community in Maine in 1915.

The second wave of Muslim immigration to the United States began after World War I (1914–1918). Once again, the majority of the Muslim immigrants were Arabs who had lived under Ottoman rule (and now found their lands administered by Britain and France following the dismantling of the Ottoman Empire). But legislation passed in the United States during the 1920s imposed numerical limits on immigration based on "national origin," and this had the effect of keeping out Muslims and others from certain areas, such as southern Europe. In the 1930s, during the Great Depression, overall immigration fell as the United States sought to exclude immigrants who might become public charges.

Immigration patterns shifted after World War II. Between 1947 and 1960, fewer people came from the Arab world. Strict quotas imposed by the Nationality Act of 1953 limited the number of people who could enter from various nations. Many Arab nations that had already dispatched large numbers of immigrants were affected by these laws. But the number of Muslims coming from Europe—especially Yugoslavia, Albania, and the Ukraine—

Lebanese Americans at a Fall River, Massachusetts, celebration of their culture. Lebanese (Christians as well as Muslims) were among the first Arabs to immigrate to the United States. Many of these early immigrants intended to return home after working and saving money, but those plans were rarely fulfilled.

increased. They were joined by a significant number of Muslims from India, where independence from Great Britain in 1947 was accompanied by a wave of Hindu-Muslim violence and the partition of the Indian subcontinent into predominantly Hindu India and predominantly Muslim Pakistan. Many of the Muslim immigrants from India were well educated and familiar with Western culture. Educational opportunities in the United States were a major attraction for this group, along with refuge from violence

The influence of Middle Eastern cultures in the United States is evident in these street scenes from Brooklyn, New York.

and religious and social discrimination.

After President Lyndon B. Johnson signed into law the Immigration and Nationality Act of 1965, which removed immigration restrictions based on national origin, Muslim immigration spiked. In addition to more Arabs, Indians, and Europeans, Muslims from Southeast Asia, Iran, Pakistan, and Africa came in significant numbers.

Conflicts spurred many Muslims to leave their homelands and move to the United States during the last decades of the 20th century. In June 1967 Israel crushed the armies of Egypt, Syria, and Jordan in what came to be called the Six-Day War, and many Palestinian Arabs were displaced from their homes in the process. Though the United States did not directly take in Palestinian refugees, many came via Jordan and Syria. A dozen years later, the Islamic Revolution in Iran, which brought to power the Ayatollah Ruhollah Khomeini, led to an upsurge in Iranian immigration to the United States. In that same year, 1979, the Soviet Union invaded Afghanistan, touching off a decade of bitter fighting that produced a stream of Afghan refugees (though relatively few came to the United States).

Devastating civil wars drove many Muslims to the United States from Lebanon, Somalia, and Sudan (the latter two countries also faced famine). Similarly, Iraqi dictator Saddam Hussein's brutal suppression of Kurdish and Shiite uprisings against his rule following the 1991 Gulf War prompted many Iraqi Kurds and Shiites to seek asylum in the United States.

The disintegration of Yugoslavia in the 1990s led to two waves of Muslim refugees. After Bosnia and Herzegovina declared its independence in 1992, a brutal, ethnically based civil war raged there for three years. The conflict claimed nearly 250,000 lives, and—in a tactic euphemistically referred to as ethnic cleansing—about a million people were driven from their homes. Most were Bosnian Muslims, more than 30,000 of whom came to the United States as refugees. Later in the decade, fighting in Kosovo—an ethnic Albanian, Muslim enclave within the Yugoslav republic of

A forensic anthropologist sifts through a mass grave believed to contain the remains of Muslims massacred during the Bosnian civil war (1992–1995). As a result of that brutal conflict, more than 30,000 Bosnian Muslim refugees came to the United States.

Serbia—displaced some 900,000 people. To prevent a humanitarian disaster, the United States agreed to accept 20,000 Kosovar refugees; other nations took in displaced Kosovars as well.

The Muslim immigrants and refugees who have come to the United States are quite diverse—not only racially, ethnically, and culturally, but also in the Islamic beliefs and traditions they hold. Some of these people are Shiites, some Sunnis. Others follow

Sufism. Still others are from offshoots of mainstream Islam, like the Druze and Ahmadiyya. As the Muslim community in the United States develops, this diversity plays an important role.

AMERICAN CONVERTS TO ISLAM

Converts add to the rich mosaic of American Islam. In the United States, most converts to Islam come from the African American community. However, Islam appeals to individuals from many different social, racial, and economic groups.

Many who have become Muslim call themselves "reverts" rather than "converts." This reflects the Islamic belief that all humans are born Muslim, aware of the oneness of God. In their view, they are not adopting a new system of belief, but just going back to one that was a part of their nature at birth.

New Muslims in the United States frequently encounter a variety of challenges. One of the more common difficulties is family rejection. Converts who come from the Judeo-Christian tradition may find that their loved ones view their embrace of Islam as a rejection of family values, even as a betrayal. And the many misconceptions about what Islam stands for only make this situation worse.

On the other hand, many new Muslims find it difficult to adjust to the Muslim community. Often they go through a period during which they feel caught between two worlds—they don't fit in with their families, and they still feel like outsiders with Muslims. Converts hoping to quietly blend into Muslim life and begin their spiritual journey are often met with unbridled enthusiasm from the Muslim community. Though many of them are still learning to practice the basic requirements of Islam, they feel pressured to adopt forms of attire and etiquette to reflect their conversion. Often this sudden and premature change in their appearances and behavior further alienates their families.

Though the situation is improving, the larger Muslim community is not always sensitive to the needs of its new members. Few programs exist that promote adjustment and understanding for converts and their non-Muslim families. In many areas there is even a shortage of basic Islam classes to help the new Muslims learn about their adopted faith. Consequently, new Muslims have formed their own support groups, particularly in bigger cities, to help them deal with the issues that accompany their decision to convert.

ISLAM BEHIND BARS

It has been estimated that more than 300,000 inmates in American prisons are converts to Islam. Many of these prisoners—following in the footsteps of Malcolm X, who discovered Islam as a young man while serving time for burglary—are African Americans. However, Hispanics and Native Americans make up a proportion of the estimated 30,000 inmates who convert to Islam annually. Islam—with its emphasis on discipline, good conduct, and reform—holds great appeal for many who have run into trouble with the law.

African American Muslim organizations have taken the lead in setting up programs to educate prisoners about Islam. In the past, many prison officials opposed these efforts, but Muslims have increasingly won the ability to freely and fully practice their faith behind bars—in large part because corrections professionals generally view Islam as a positive influence on prisoners. Thus many prisons have Muslim chaplains who counsel and educate inmates on the teachings of Islam. Some prisons allow inmates to attend Arabic and Qur'an classes. It is also common to see Muslims gathered in prayer in prison yards or rooms assigned to them for Friday prayer. Increasingly, corrections facilities are also catering to Muslim dietary laws and providing *halal* food and meals during Ramadan. In addition, many Muslim inmates can now observe prophetic traditions such as keeping a beard and wearing some forms of clothing associated with Muslim culture.

An Iranian-born imam speaks at a gathering of American Shiites. About one in five Muslims in the United States belongs to the Shiite sect; as is the case worldwide, Sunnis form the largest Muslim group in America.

THE SUNNI AND SHIITE COMMUNITIES IN THE UNITED STATES

Islam in the United States is marked not only by the racial, ethnic, and cultural diversity of believers, but also by the mixture of approaches and ideas. The American Muslim population is composed of a number of distinct communities. Sunnis and Shiites, who make up the largest of these communities, are commonly said to represent mainstream Islam. These mainstream groups are joined by several minor groups.

Sunnis make up the largest proportion of the overall American Muslim population. They also represent the widest scope of ethnicities—coming from the Middle East, Central Asia, Southeast Asia, Europe, and Africa. Most converts to Islam in the United States are also Sunnis. The majority of Shiites, who constitute about one-fifth of the U.S. Muslim population, come from Iran, Iraq, Pakistan, Afghanistan, and India.

Sunnis and Shiites share core beliefs. Both groups are guided by the Qur'an and the Sunna (the body of Islamic custom drawn from the example of Muhammad's words and deeds). There are certain differences in religious practices, however. For example, while both groups follow the five pillars, there are slight variations in the way that they put them into practice. Shiite tradition allows the five daily prayers to be combined into three prayer times (a person who chooses to do this offers the morning prayer as usual but combines the two afternoon prayers and the two night prayers). By contrast, Sunni Muslims combine their prayers only in extenuating circumstances, such as during long-distance travel. Shiite Muslims are also required to pay an additional tax called the *khums*. This tax, which is one-fifth of their earnings, is used to support their community.

On a doctrinal level, Shiites believe that in addition to the Qur'an and the Sunna, Muslims have been guided by a line of divinely inspired leaders (Imams) beginning with Ali, the cousin of Muhammad. In addition to the religious holidays celebrated by all Muslims, Shiite mosques pay special attention to such occasions as Ashura, a solemn remembrance of the murder of Hussain (son of Ali and grandson of the Prophet) who is considered an Imam.

In many major cities in the United States, Shiites have established their own mosques and centers to address their specific religious needs. In smaller cities and towns, however, people from both the Sunni and the Shia traditions frequently worship together and attend the same mosques. Most try not to focus on their differences. Their families socialize with one another, and children from both groups attend the same Sunday schools. Shiites in these small cities simply practice the special requirements and observances of their faith separate from their Sunni neighbors.

But it cannot be said that Shiite-Sunni tensions—which exist throughout the Islamic world—are absent from the American Muslim community. One reason, of course, is that Sunnis and

Shiites sometimes bring sectarian disagreements and grievances against each other with them when they immigrate to the United States. In Iraq, for example, Shiites constitute a majority, but under the regime of Saddam Hussein they were discriminated against and, at times, brutally repressed by the Sunni minority. In the United States disagreements between Sunnis and Shiites have never been as bitter. Still, a divide does exist, despite the efforts of American Muslims to bring the mainstream communities together.

One development that seems to have increased Sunni-Shiite cooperation in the United States is the terrorist attacks of September 11, 2001. In the aftermath of the attacks, Sunni and Shiite Muslims alike found themselves under a cloud of suspicion and, on occasion, were the victims of intimidation and violence. In seeking to educate the American public about Islam, Shiite scholars—including many of the best-known Islamic authorities in the United States—spoke up for the entire Muslim community. Similarly, Sunni spokesmen have made it a point to include the Shiite community when representing Islam to the American public.

SUFISM IN THE UNITED STATES

Driving past the adobe structures of Dar al Islam in Abiquiu, New Mexico, one can glimpse a Sufi community in the American Southwest. The mosque and surrounding buildings are meant to be a spiritual neighborhood. Age-old Sufi traditions inspire the small group of Muslims who live there.

Sufism is a mystical tradition that emphasizes inner spirituality. Because it is a special approach to religion and not a religion in itself, it is practiced by Sunnis and Shiites in the mainstream Muslim population. Sufism, which helped spread Islam throughout Asia and Africa, also attracts converts to Islam in the United States, who join traditional Sufi groups or orders called *tariqas*, or paths. Typically, the order centers on a spiritual leader called a *shaykh* (master).

In addition to fulfilling the basic requirements of Islam, Sufi orders also assemble for meditations in remembrance of God; such remembrance is called *dhikr*. Though each order has its own unique ritual, in a typical *dhikr* session members might sit in a circle and rhythmically recite the names of God.

The majority of Sufi orders throughout history have integrated their Sufi traditions and approaches with orthodox Islamic practice. But a few groups have been criticized for not adhering to the basic requirements of Islam—for example, because they have not practiced the five pillars and other outward forms of worship but instead have focused on inner worship and various forms of meditation taking the form of music and dance, as in the case of the Whirling Dervishes. A few American Sufi groups that are loosely based in Islamic Sufi tradition are not considered Islamic. The Sufi Order of the West, the largest of these organizations, combines New Age practices as well as rituals from religions such as Hinduism and Buddhism. Increasingly, however, such uniquely Western groups are being overshadowed by more traditional Sufi groups that have long histories in the Islamic world.

Two views of Dar al Islam, Abiquiu, New Mexico.

DRUZE AND AHMADIYYA

In addition to the mainstream Muslim sects, the United States is home to members of the Druze and Ahmadiyya sects, though their numbers are relatively small. Many mainstream Muslims do not consider either of these sects part of Islam.

The Druze sect, which began around 1000 C.E. as an offshoot of Shia Islam, is very secretive about its practices. The Druze do not accept converts or permit marriage outside their faith.

Like many early Arab immigrants, the Druze—who are primarily of Lebanese and Syrian descent—have blended easily into American society. Recently, however, some members of the American Druze community have been trying to reinvigorate their traditions and have begun claiming more of a connection to the larger Islamic community.

The Ahmadiyya sect, an offshoot of Sunni Islam, was founded in Punjab, India, during the 1800s by Hazrat Mirza Ghulam Ahmad, who claimed to receive divine revelation. According to most reports, he saw himself as a messenger who was sent to renew and reform the practice of Islam. Some Muslims maintain that he actually claimed to be a prophet—which, if true, would contradict the Islamic belief that Muhammad was the last of the prophets. This is the reason Sunni Muslims in the United States do not consider the Ahmadiyya sect part of Islam. The Ahmadis, however, insist that they represent the true Islam.

The Ahmadiyya movement came to the United States in 1920. Unlike the Druze, the Ahmadis actively seek to spread their message and win converts. Ahmadis, who mainly claim Indian and Pakistani roots, have had a fair degree of success in attracting African Americans. They even produce literature for the general Muslim public. From their current headquarters in Washington, D.C., they publish and distribute literature to spread their faith. They continue to grow in number and have centers in more than 50 North American cities.

The flag of the Nation of Islam is held aloft as a crowd listens to a speech during the Million Family March, Washington, D.C., October 16, 2000. The Nation of Islam, which has combined Muslim religious practices with a call for black empowerment and responsibility, has attracted many followers from the African American community.

African Americans and Islam

B y the time the Civil War broke out in 1861, slavery had existed for three centuries in the United States (and, before the American Revolution, in the colonies). A cruel and dehumanizing institution, slavery had not merely robbed blacks of their freedom; it had extinguished their African identities, their cultural traditions, and their religious beliefs.

Unfortunately, the abolition of slavery in the United States did not bring equality to blacks. In the South, a system of segregation (and de facto discrimination against blacks) developed; referred to as Jim Crow, it received the legal blessing of the United States Supreme Court in the 1892 *Plessy v. Ferguson* decision. African Americans who "forgot their place" were subject to lynching, and typically the perpetrators were not punished. Though supposedly guaranteed the right to vote by the 15th Amendment, ratified in 1870, blacks found their political voice silenced by discriminatory measures such as poll taxes and literacy tests. Even in the North, racism was rampant and blacks were often treated as second-class citizens.

Faced with continuing discrimination, inequality, and hostility from white America, black leaders in the early decades of the 20th century began searching for ways to improve the plight of the African American community. Some, recognizing that slavery had robbed blacks in the United States of their identity and power as a people, saw a need for African Americans to reconnect with their African roots (or even to return to Africa or to unite with African peoples). It was in looking to Africa, and toward their West African origins, that some blacks in the United States rediscovered Islam. As the 20th century progressed, Islam would become a powerful force in the African American community, though for many believers it would take a form somewhat different from that found elsewhere in the Islamic world.

THE SEARCH FOR IDENTITY AND THE MOORISH SCIENCE TEMPLE

In 1913 an African American named Noble Drew Ali started a movement called the Moorish Science Temple of America. Ali, who was born Timothy Drew, believed that all Africans were Asiatic or Moorish descendants. Refusing labels such as colored and Negro, he called for blacks to shed the slave identities forced upon them by whites and to adopt new names and new appearances to reflect their noble lineage. While promoting black unity, he also pushed African Americans toward social and economic independence.

Convinced he was a prophet (which, of course, separates his movement from mainstream Islam), Ali wrote the *Holy Koran of the Moorish Science Temple of America*. The book has no similarity to the Qur'an. After Ali's death in 1929, his organization continued to grow. Today, the Moorish Science Temple is based in Chicago. Most of its members are African American and continue to adopt Moorish names and traditional clothing. The Moorish Science Temple has received public recognition for its social work in the African American community.

THE NATION OF ISLAM

Between 1910 and 1930, more than a million blacks from the rural South—hoping to escape discrimination and poverty—moved to the cities of the North in what is known as the Great Migration. Though many found relatively well paying industrial jobs, often the adjustment to urban living was difficult (like other ethnic minorities, blacks typically lived in inner-city ghettos). Nor was the North free from racial intolerance. And, with

Elijah Muhammad, born in 1897 to former slaves in Sandersville, Georgia, led the Nation of Islam from 1934 until his death in 1975.

the stock market crash in 1929 and the onset of the Great Depression, hundreds of thousands of blacks, like other Americans, lost their jobs.

In 1930, in the midst of this bleak situation, a self-proclaimed "prophet who had a startling message of African American identity and destiny" appeared in Detroit, where he founded the Lost-Found Nation of Islam. The origins of W. D. Fard (also known as Wallace Fard Muhammad and Wali Farad) are somewhat mysterious. He may have been born in Mecca around 1877, though precisely when he immigrated to the United States is unknown; followers described him as Arab or, more specifically, as Palestinian. In any event, Fard preached a message of black unity and supremacy to the African Americans—mainly migrants from the South—with whom he came in contact in the course of his job as a door-to-door silk peddler. Fard encouraged his followers to clean up their lifestyles—to stop drinking, smoking, and engaging in immoral behavior. He said that Christianity was the religion of slaveholders, and in order to break with their past, he instructed his followers to drop their last names and thus their slave identities. In place of their last names, he gave each of them an X to represent the identity that had been stolen from them during slavery. Soon the Nation of Islam had a sizable following in the African American ghettos of Detroit. Then, in 1934, Fard disappeared as mysteriously as he had appeared.

At that time his closest disciple, Elijah Muhammad, became the new leader of the Nation of Islam. He expanded its reach to Chicago and, in the years to follow, to cities throughout the United States.

The Nation of Islam adopted many aspects of Muslim culture and practice, including prayer, almsgiving, dietary restrictions, and even Arabic names. Yet many of its core teachings and values are opposed to those of orthodox Islam. For example, Elijah Muhammad claimed that he was a prophet and that W. D. Fard was Allah. He called white men devils and claimed that blacks are a superior race destined to rule the earth, contradicting the Islamic belief in the equality of all people before God. Thus orthodox Muslims came to regard the Nation of Islam as a manifestation of black nationalism rather than a true Islamic movement.

A Turn Toward Mainstream Islam

If the founders of the Nation of Islam, W. D. Fard and Elijah Muhammad, drew inspiration from orthodox Islam but ultimately diverged from it, two later figures would journey from prominent roles in the Nation of Islam to an embrace of mainstream Islam. The more famous of the two was born in 1925 in Omaha, Nebraska. His birth name was Malcolm Little, but the world would come to know him better by the name he took upon converting to the Nation of Islam: Malcolm X.

Malcolm X, photographed in 1964, the year he broke with the Nation of Islam and made the hajj. The pilgrimage to Mecca transformed Malcolm's outlook, leading to his abandonment of black separatism and his embrace of mainstream, orthodox Islam.

That conversion took place while he was serving a prison term for burglary. During his time behind bars, Malcolm—who possessed a keen intellect but was a high school dropout—read widely on social history, politics, and philosophy. By the time of his release in 1952, he was a firm proponent of black supremacy and separatism.

A charismatic and knowledgeable speaker, Malcolm soon caught the eye of Elijah Muhammad, who made him a minister and spokesman for the Nation of Islam. His powerful oratory increased his popularity and facilitated his rise within the ranks of the Nation of Islam's leaders. But his popularity also caused jealousy within the Nation's hierarchy, and open conflict arose when Malcolm denounced Elijah Muhammad's sexual infidelities. By early 1964 Malcolm had broken with the Nation of Islam and started his own group, the Muslim Mosque, Inc.

In 1964 Malcolm also went on the hajj, an experience that would transform his entire outlook. While on the pilgrimage to Mecca he was exposed, for the first time in his life, to the diversity of the Islamic community. As he later revealed, he met "blonde-haired, blued-eyed men I could call my brothers." He returned to the United States determined to continue fighting racial injustice, but he no longer believed in black supremacy and racial separation. He had embraced mainstream, orthodox Islam. To mark the transformation, he changed his name to El Hajj Malik el-Shabazz.

Unfortunately his life would soon be cut short. On February 21, 1965, he was gunned down at a New York speaking engagement. Three members of the Nation of Islam were later convicted of the killing.

After the 1975 death of Elijah Muhammad, leadership of the Nation of Islam passed to his son Wallace D. Muhammad. Since his childhood Wallace Muhammad had been attracted to the teachings of orthodox Islam, and he had studied Arabic and the Qur'an. Influenced by his studies of Islamic spirituality, he was skeptical of the Nation of Islam's approach. Particularly troublesome to him were its notions of black superiority. As a

The charismatic and controversial Louis Farrakhan became the leader of the reorganized Nation of Islam in the late 1970s.

teenager, he began to question other fundamental teachings of the Nation. Looking at a portrait of the fair-skinned W. D. Fard, he wondered why "a man looking so white was supposed to be black and a black god." Because he continually challenged the Nation's beliefs, and because he maintained close ties to Malcolm X, Wallace Muhammad was expelled from the organization. He was welcomed back just a year before his father's death.

Gradually he steered the Nation of Islam toward orthodox Islam. To conform to the Islamic principles in the *shahada*, he declared that W. D. Fard was not divine and Elijah Muhammad was not a prophet. Rather, he simply credited both men with advancing the state of black society in the United States through the introduction of Islam to black Americans. He renounced the Nation's black supremacist orientation. He changed his name to Warith Deen Mohammed and the organization's name first to the World Community of al-Islam in the West, then to the American Muslim Mission. He welcomed white believers. Finally, in 1985, he officially dissolved the organization so that followers could join the worldwide community of orthodox Muslims. His followers are members of the mainstream Sunni community.

Today, Mohammed heads the Muslim American Society, a non-profit social, cultural, and educational organization. He is recognized by the international Muslim community as a key Muslim American leader. He is also a frequent speaker at Muslim conferences and conventions. At these forums he often speaks about a need for a uniquely American Islamic scholarship. He and his colleagues also continue to provide important services, including high-quality schools and educational programs, to all African Americans.

While Warith Deen Mohammed was steering his followers toward Sunni Islam, another leader, Louis Farrakhan, picked up the mantle of Elijah Muhammad. After breaking with Warith Deen Mohammed, Farrakhan assumed leadership of a reestablished Nation of Islam, which stayed closer to the founding principles of the original group. He attracted many converts with his commanding presence, soaring oratory, and powerful message of black self-improvement and self-reliance. In 1995 his charisma attracted hundreds of thousands of African Americans from across the United States to the "Million Man March" in Washington, D.C. That event was essentially a call for African American men to accept responsibility for their actions and to commit themselves to improving the black community.

But many Americans consider Farrakhan a divisive figure, even a racist. And despite his periodic overtures to the worldwide Muslim community, most orthodox Muslims insist that the Nation of Islam is not an Islamic movement. They point to its continued exclusion of nonblacks, as well as various other teachings that are opposed to the Islam of the Qur'an.

Joseph Howar, a Jerusalem-born contractor, poses in front of the Islamic Center in Washington, D.C. Fulfilling a lifelong dream, Howar—a devout Muslim—helped build the center, which was completed in 1957.

American Muslim Life

A merican Muslims are constantly searching for ways to meet their religious requirements in the midst of the bustle of American life. In most Islamic countries prayers are integrated into daily activities. While Muslims in other countries rely on the *adhan* to call them to prayer, American Muslims have had to resort to other, less public forms of scheduling. Monthly and yearly time schedules for the five daily prayers are published regularly by local mosques and Islamic organizations. Various Internet sites and computer software also calculate prayer times based on geographic location. Because the sun rises and sets at different times throughout the U.S. time zones, prayer times differ slightly from place to place. It is important to note that prayers do not have to be offered at one specific point in time. Rather, each prayer has a window of opportunity. For example, the time for *fajr*, or early-morning, prayer might begin at 5:30 A.M. and finish by 7:00, just before the sun rises. In order to remember prayer, American Muslims mostly rely on their own memory. Some homes have special clocks or computer programs that play a recording of the *adhan* at the beginning of each prayer window.

Prayer at the workplace poses several challenges. At least one of the prayers falls right in the middle of the workday. Muslims who have their own business or have a private office often take time out of their schedule to pray. The entire process, including the ablution and the prayer itself, takes an average of only 15 minutes. Nonetheless, Muslims who work in businesses and industries that have tight schedules are often unable to take additional time for prayer. They usually make up their missed prayers when they get home.

As for the Friday prayer, the number of American Muslims who attend this weekly event continues to grow. Many businesses allow their Muslim employees to take a few hours every Friday to fulfill their spiritual obligations. To compensate for missed time, some Muslims put in a few extra hours of work at other times during the week. Many who can't attend a mosque prayer participate in smaller group prayers held in rented rooms that are close to their workplaces. Prayers are even held in a few businesses around the country. Because Friday prayer can officially be conducted with as few as three people, businesses with a large enough number of Muslims hold their own congregations. Eager to see more attendees, Muslims have even modified the Friday prayers to better accommodate working people. The *khutbas*, or sermons, that precede the prayer are shortened, as are the prayers themselves. Often, communities also sell bag lunches and snacks after the prayer. In a particularly efficient service, a person can go to Friday prayer, eat, and be back before the end of his or her lunch hour.

MOSQUES AND COMMUNITY CENTERS

Mosques have changed since Muhammad and his companions built the first in Medina during the seventh century. Throughout the Islamic world, these buildings of worship are emblems of the

A mosque and Islamic school in Brooklyn, New York.

spiritual and artistic zeal of Muslims, from the domes and intricate tile work of Iranian mosques to the sprawling architectural spectacles of Turkey.

In the United States, mosques have evolved to suit American life. Some imitate the architectural styles and structures traditionally found in mosques around the world. But domes, minarets, and arches are costly to build. Unlike the rest of the Islamic world, which often gets public funding for mosques, Muslim communities in the United States rely on donations and often cannot afford the classical building styles. As a result, newer mosques tend to be more functional, and most do not have domes or minarets.

The first permanent mosque in the United States was built in

Mosques are more than just places to worship; they also serve as community centers. Among the many programs American mosques typically sponsor are Sunday school classes where young children learn about their faith.

1934 by Syrian immigrants in Cedar Rapids, Iowa. Before they had their own mosque, however, they—like many communities since—prayed and congregated in rented halls. Many Muslims even had their first gatherings in space rented from Christian churches. Though many small communities from low-income areas still rent space or buy old buildings to convert into mosques, some of the larger communities have built their own structures. Growing communities have also realized that Muslims need their own space—places where they can go for religious, social, and cultural activities. Consequently, most American mosques are more than just places to pray. Instead, they are community centers that serve a variety of purposes. They are places to learn, to socialize, and to celebrate community events. These centers commonly feature Sunday schools for children, gymnasiums, and cafeterias and event halls. Some even house full-time Muslim schools. In urban areas, many community centers also offer career counseling and English classes for new immigrants.

Though a large percentage of Muslims belong to community centers and organizations, some choose to fulfill their religious obligations in other ways. In fact, many committed and religious Muslims don't belong to a mosque community. Of those who do, some regularly go to the mosque for prayers and weekly study meetings. Others choose to attend on Fridays for Friday prayer or only on special events and holidays.

IMAMS

According to Islamic teaching, prayer can be led by anyone who is knowledgeable in the Qur'an and well respected by the community. Islam, unlike Christianity and Judaism, does not have a separate religious clergy. Religious rituals and sermons can be directed by anyone who has enough knowledge. Of course, in the early days of Islam, the typical believer was far more educated in Qur'anic and religious sciences than are most of today's Muslims.

In the United States the person who leads prayer, the imam, is usually chosen by the rest of the community. In smaller communities, a different person might lead each of the prayers. However, large communities often appoint full-time imams. In many cases,

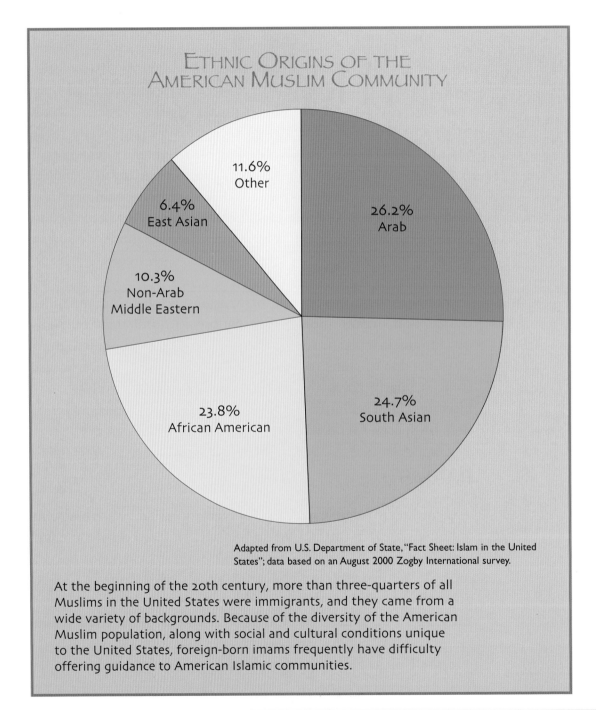

ETHNIC ORIGINS OF THE
AMERICAN MUSLIM COMMUNITY

11.6%
Other

6.4%
East Asian

10.3%
Non-Arab
Middle Eastern

26.2%
Arab

23.8%
African American

24.7%
South Asian

Adapted from U.S. Department of State, "Fact Sheet: Islam in the United States"; data based on an August 2000 Zogby International survey.

At the beginning of the 20th century, more than three-quarters of all Muslims in the United States were immigrants, and they came from a wide variety of backgrounds. Because of the diversity of the American Muslim population, along with social and cultural conditions unique to the United States, foreign-born imams frequently have difficulty offering guidance to American Islamic communities.

Muslim communities bring their full-time imams from overseas.

The role of the imam in the United States continues to evolve. In addition to leading prayers, American imams often fill roles that are taken on by others in traditional Muslim communities. In other parts of the Islamic world, shaykhs and Muslim scholars with specialized knowledge of the Qur'an, the Sunna, and Islamic law address the religious questions and concerns of believers in the community. But because of a lack of trained Islamic scholars in the United States, imams frequently fill this role, or American Muslims turn to foreign scholars for guidance.

Unfortunately, foreign scholars and imams who have come from another country often have trouble relating to American Muslims—first, because of a language barrier, and second, because they are largely unfamiliar with issues unique to the American Muslim community. Many communities have recognized the need for well-prepared imams who possess good communication skills and are aware of the challenges that American Muslims face within their families, in the workplace, between each other, and with non-Muslims. Imams must also be trained to deal with young Muslims who face issues of growing up, going to school, dating, and substance abuse. And as they are called on as counselors to advise members of their community on issues of marriage, divorce, and children, imams will clearly need to take advantage of the growing number of young professional counselors and social workers within the Muslim community. Finally, because people look to imams for religious education, imams must have a substantial knowledge of Islam. To meet these needs, several imam-training programs have been established in the United States. These include chaplain programs to train imams to provide religious services for the military and in prisons.

CHARITY

Muslims get an idea of how to spend their alms tax, or *zakat*, from the Qur'an, which points to general categories of needy people, such as orphans. But who specifically receives the charity is left up to the individual donors and the communities. Traditionally, Islamic countries have had institutions responsible for collecting the *zakat* and ensuring that it goes to the neediest people. Muslims in the United States are developing organizations with a similar function. In local communities, mosques and Islamic centers collect the alms tax and then distribute the funds. In general, needy members of the immediate community receive priority. Several national charities also specialize in collecting and distributing *zakat*. For the most part, however, these groups focus on international need.

Whether *zakat* should focus on the Muslim community in the United States or the international Muslim community is a much-debated topic among American Muslims. Immigrant Muslims are torn on this issue. Because they typically still feel strong ties to their country of birth, they often choose to send their alms tax to needy people there. Even Muslims born in the United States who consider themselves fully American often send *zakat* money to unfortunate Muslims in countries ravaged by famine, war, or natural disasters, such as Somalia, Bosnia and Herzegovina, or Bangladesh.

In addition to the required *zakat*, Muslims are highly encouraged to give voluntary charity, *sadaqa*. Many donate anonymously, wishing it to be an act of devotion to God. However, communities also hold public charity events and drives, believing that competing for good causes is socially beneficial. Mosques and community centers often have collection boxes where people can regularly deposit their donations. Special efforts are also made to help Muslims in other parts of the world. During wars, famines, and other natural disasters, some communities cooperate with larger relief agencies by collecting food, clothing, and blankets to send abroad. Locally, mosques and community centers run food drives and soup kitchens. Efforts like these often coincide with the month of Ramadan, when there is an increased awareness of the needs of others.

RAMADAN

Almost every Muslim looks forward to the holy month of Ramadan, when the faithful believe the Qur'an was revealed. Even for nonpracticing Muslims, this month has a special significance. Throughout the Islamic world, it is a time of peace and heightened spirituality, when Muslims have the opportunity to practice self-control, patience, and charity.

Ramadan is the ninth lunar month on the Islamic calendar. According to Islamic teaching, Ramadan begins when at least one person physically sights the crescent moon that indicates the start of the month. Of course, Muslims are now able to accurately calculate the cycles of the moon using modern technology. Whether or not it is still necessary for a person to actually see the moon is a hotly debated issue in the Islamic world—especially in the United States. Some Muslims interpret the traditional moon sighting laws literally: if the law says a person must see the moon, they insist, then technology is irrelevant. Others believe that the scientific calculations equal human vision and are more accurate. As a result of the difference in opinion, those who go by calculations and those who go by physical sighting often start and end Ramadan on different days. Depending on their moon sighting opinions, Muslims may fast one to two days apart. Whatever their view, many American Muslim families still make a special outing on the expected night of the crescent moon to see if they can spy it for themselves.

Because the Islamic calendar is based on lunar cycles and its year is approximately 354 days long, Ramadan shifts back about 11 days each year with respect to the Western, or Gregorian, calendar. When Ramadan falls in the winter, the days are very short, so the required fasting during daylight hours is somewhat easier. However, when Ramadan falls during summer, Muslims face long, hot days of up to 15 hours without food or drink, including water. The month of fasting lasts between 28 and 30 days and ends with the sighting of the new moon.

To sustain them during the day's fast, Muslims wake up before dawn to eat a small meal. Predawn meals differ according to a person's cultural background. A Pakistani might eat a regular dinner meal with bread or rice and various accompanying dishes, whereas an Egyptian family might have a bean dip with bread; an American family might have a sweet meal of pancakes and syrup. A short while before the first light of the sun, Muslims stop eating and drinking and begin their fast. After performing the morning prayer, many Muslims go back to sleep until it is time to wake up for work or school.

Refraining from food and drink is not the only obligation during the daylight hours of Ramadan. For faithful Muslims, several other physical activities, such as sex and smoking, are off-limits during this time as well. And throughout the month, not simply during daylight hours, Muslims try to abstain from negative behaviors such as arguing, name-calling, losing their tempers, and gossiping.

At sunset, many Muslims break their fast as did the Prophet Muhammad, with a date and some water. This is usually followed by a small snack and then by the evening prayer. Following the prayer, families often sit down for a large meal. As Ramadan is meant to be a month where individuals can practice self-control and empathy for those less fortunate, eating lavish meals and wasting food are discouraged. Still, some of the most elaborate meals in the Islamic world are cooked during this month.

Each Islamic country has its own special customs and traditions during Ramadan. The streets of Egypt, for example, are aglow with festive lamps, and markets throughout the Middle East close early for breakfast and then reopen later in the night. In the United States, Ramadan traditions are still developing. Muslims incorporate small traditions from around the Islamic world in their own homes. Parents strive to make Ramadan and other Muslim holidays more appealing and festive for their children. Inundated with Christmas and Chanukah traditions at school, they often look for special celebrations of their own. One

Ramadan tradition that is seen more in the United States than in most Islamic countries is frequent community dinners. Because feeding others during Ramadan is considered a reward-filled deed, many families invite one another to their homes for Ramadan meals. In addition to feeding friends and family, mosques throughout the United States run soup kitchens or sponsor food drives for the poor.

Across the world, mosque attendance is also higher during Ramadan than at any other time of the year. American mosques host weekly dinners where community members can break their fasts together. Following the last prayer of the day, mosques also hold the *tarawih* prayers. To lead the special night prayers, many mosques bring imams from other countries. People enjoy praying the long prayers with these imams, who are often trained in beautiful Qur'anic recitation.

Laylat al-Qadr, the Night of Power, falls during the last 10 days of Ramadan. On this occasion, mosques are also open to Muslims who wish to stay all night praying and reading the Qur'an. However, many choose to observe this night at home with their families. The Night of Power is the night when Muslims believe that God completed the Qur'anic revelation. Worship on this night, according to the Qur'an, is worth the prayers of a thousand months. Because of the Qur'an's significance to this month, many Muslims also make an effort to read and study it more often.

In recent years, non-Muslims in the United States have become more aware of Ramadan. In 2001 President George W. Bush hosted a Ramadan breakfast at the White House. He also released a press statement in recognition of the holy Islamic month. In addition, some television and radio stations air public service announcements with Ramadan greetings.

DIETARY RESTRICTIONS

Like Jews, Muslims have specific rules regarding their diet. Because of health concerns, the Qur'an prohibits Muslims from

In a sign of how sizable the Muslim community has become, this McDonald's in Dearborn offers *halal* food.

consuming pork or alcohol. Among the reasons alcohol is forbidden is that it impairs good judgment and mental clarity. Besides not drinking it, some Muslims avoid going to restaurants and homes that serve alcohol. They also shun jobs where they will have to sell alcohol.

Muslims must also be careful when they shop, since pork by-products are ingredients in many packaged foods sold in the United States. In addition to avoiding pork in food, many Muslims also stay clear of cosmetics and soaps that contain pork by-products. Some Muslim groups research and publish lists of products and their ingredients to help Muslims make informed shopping decisions.

Halal foods are those that Muslims are allowed to eat. This includes most everything other than pork and alcohol. However, in order for meat to be considered *halal*, it must be specially prepared. In the ritual, God's name is first pronounced over the animal, and then it is slaughtered in a way that is considered most humane for the animal and most healthful for humans. Specially prepared lamb, beef, or poultry is available in small *halal* markets throughout the country. Several states actually have laws, similar to kosher laws, requiring certification for anything that is sold with a *halal* label. Before *halal* meat was readily available, American Muslims used to look for meat certified as kosher for Jewish people. To make life easier, the Qur'an allows Muslims to eat meat slaughtered by Christians and Jews, People of the Book. Eating *halal* meat only is a personal decision that many American Muslims make.

CELEBRATIONS AND FESTIVALS

Along with the rest of the Islamic world, American Muslims celebrate two major Islamic holidays—Eid al-Fitr and Eid al-Adha. "The Feast of Breaking the Fast," Eid al-Fitr is a three-day holiday that begins the day after Ramadan ends. It is marked by a festival of food. On the morning of Eid al-Fitr, Muslims wake up and symbolically break their fast as they did the previous evening, often with a date fruit and water. Then they eat a breakfast featuring Eid foods from various cultures. Afterward, Muslim families attend a large congregational prayer. Before the prayer, each Muslim is required to give *zakat al fitr*, one meal's worth of money (an average of 7 to 10 dollars) for the needy. The Eid prayer itself has a special format that differs slightly from a regular prayer and is offered in addition to the other five prayers. The imam follows up the prayer with a *khutba*, a sermon that often reflects upon lessons learned during Ramadan or upon a subject of social relevance.

Eid al-Adha, "the Feast of the Sacrifice," is a more substantial observance. It begins on the last day of the hajj in Mecca and continues for seven days. Both the pilgrimage and Eid al-Adha honor the story of Abraham. Eid al-Adha specifically commemorates God's blissful intervention in providing Abraham with a ram to sacrifice in place of his son Ishmael. On this holiday, as on Eid al-Fitr, Muslims attend a large special prayer that is followed by a sermon. Typically, they also sacrifice animals and distribute the meat in their community, especially to the needy.

American Muslims spend both Eid holidays visiting with relatives and friends and engaging in community activities. As their families grow, they are trying to make Eid observances a pride-filled experience for their children. So, according to worldwide traditions, many adults and children wear new clothing to celebrate the occasion. Children from some cultures also receive Eid money. Just as in the Christmas and Chanukah traditions, many Muslims exchange Eid gifts. Community carnivals and picnics make the festivities even more memorable for youngsters. To promote the value of social welfare, many Muslims also make special efforts during both Eids to provide meals for the poor.

As part of the effort to promote American awareness about Islam, Muslims are pushing for national recognition of Eid al-Fitr and Eid al-Adha. In 2001 the United States Postal Service issued a special Eid stamp that featured art by a prominent Muslim American calligrapher, Mohamed Zakariya. Well received by Muslims and non-Muslims alike, the stamp has since been reissued. A similar effort is under way to get American educational institutions to recognize Islamic holidays just as they recognize Jewish and Christian observances. Some school districts have included Eid al-Fitr and Eid al-Adha on their yearly calendar. Upon request, Muslim students are excused from school on those days.

People from various Muslim cultures also observe other Islamic occasions. Some Muslims celebrate Mawlid al-Nabi, the birthday of the prophet Muhammad. Shiite Muslims also celebrate Ashura

Muslim families typically celebrate Eid al-Fitr, "the Feast of Breaking the Fast," with a festival of foods from different Islamic cultures.

in memory of the murder of the Prophet's grandson Hussain. Another notable occasion that is commemorated is al-Isra' wal-Miraj. The Qur'an describes this event as a night upon which Muhammad rose to the heavens on a miraculous voyage from Mecca to Jerusalem.

Although the community of Muslims in the United States is extremely diverse racially, culturally, ethnically, and even politically, all believers are unified by the Qur'an, and understanding Arabic is seen as essential to a true appreciation of the holy book. Here an African American Muslim student practices writing the Arabic script.

Family, Society, and Culture

Muslims are now welcoming first, second, and even third generations into American Muslim life. Though some immigrants continue to cling to their native cultures, more American Muslims are focusing their energy on creating an Islamic tradition in the United States. Family is central to this effort. Developing family traditions that meet Islamic standards, agree with the cultural sensitivities of immigrants, and are adaptable to American life is challenging. But, as families face the cycle of life, they improvise. Relying on the Qur'an and the traditions of the Prophet, Muslims are developing a culture that is American and Islamic at the same time.

Birth

Although Muslims believe that every baby is born Muslim, there are no guarantees that they will grow up to be faithful to Islam. Especially in the United States, where their children are surrounded by social pressures and other spiritual paths, Muslim parents often worry that their children will not maintain their religion. Hoping to give their children a good start in life, Muslims introduce their children to Islam as soon as they are born. Some Muslim women even believe that babies in the womb are affected by the sound of the Qur'an or by the rhythmic motions of the five daily prayers.

Birth itself is an especially spiritual event for Muslim families. Babies are considered not just a blessing, but also a sign of God's generosity and power. Moments after a baby is born, a close relative or friend softly calls the *adhan* in each of the newborn's ears. This tradition goes back to the Prophet. Though it is mostly a symbolic gesture, it gives babies their first introduction to the basic beliefs of Islam. The person who makes the *adhan* often holds a special place in the heart of the child and the family. For reasons that are attributed to good health and hygiene, male babies are circumcised just as in the Jewish tradition.

Many American Muslims follow up the birth of a child with a special celebration called *aqiqa*. As a gesture of thanks to God, families sacrifice a sheep, cow, or camel and then feed their community and friends. This is the only birth celebration that mainstream Muslims agree upon. A small number of American Muslims from some cultures and viewpoints look down on regular birthday celebrations, which they say celebrate people rather than God. Most Muslims, however, accept birthdays as an appropriate celebration. As a compromise, many parents take birthdays as an opportunity to teach their children to thank God for giving them life and good health. As it is an American custom, they also allow their children to have parties and presents.

CARING FOR THE ELDERLY

Both the Qur'an and the Prophet emphasized the importance of caring for the elderly. In Islamic teaching, it is the responsibility of each individual to care for and honor his or her parents as they age. Mothers in particular have a special status. According to one tradition, paradise lies at the mother's feet, and therefore a person who wishes the good favor of God should put extra effort into honoring and caring for his or her mother.

But Muslims are required to feed, shelter, care for, show mercy toward, and love all the aging members of their community. Accordingly, Muslim societies have traditionally taken good care of their elderly. Public organizations and extended-family living both contributed to this good care.

Within the American Muslim community, as in the wider society, many elderly men and women go to live with their children when they are no longer able to live alone. Grandparents are prized in Muslim homes because they provide support and help to raise children. According to the Islamic ideal, when the elderly are no longer able to take care of themselves, they should live with, and be cared for, by their children. However, some elderly Muslims, like many American senior citizens, find themselves alone and live out their days in nursing homes or retirement facilities.

DEATH

"From God we have come, and to God we will return." Upon hearing of someone's death, Muslims utter these words. No matter what the circumstances, Muslims view death as a natural return to their creator, and they take special steps in preparing the bodies of the deceased for this return. In Muslim lands, specific people, much like morticians, are trained to prepare bodies for burial. However, in the United States, ordinary members of the community, men and women, are trained to cleanse and wrap the bodies in the Islamic way. In this special ritual, bodies are washed in a sequence much like the ablution for prayer. They are neither embalmed nor dressed up. Rather, they are wrapped very simply in white, organic cloth, which is often scented with a sweet perfume. Sometimes, the prepared body is taken to the mosque, where Muslims gather for a special funeral prayer called *jinaza* (or *janaza*). This prayer can also be performed at the burial site.

According to Islamic tradition, Muslims should be buried within a day of their death. Bodies are buried facing Mecca, directly in the earth without a coffin (though this is not permitted in the United States), and typically with only a small grave marker. Compared with typical American funerals, Muslim burials are simpler and cost less.

MEN AND WOMEN

In the Qur'anic worldview, men and women have complementary roles—different but equally important functions within the family and in society. As with everything, Muslims look to the example of the prophet Muhammad for direction on proper conduct for both men and women, especially regarding their interactions with members of the opposite sex. Nevertheless, Muslims hold varying opinions on this matter. Many of these differences are more culturally than religiously based.

In some traditional Muslim cultures, the activities of men and women are completely segregated. Even during group prayers, the two genders pray in separate rooms. Such norms of segregation are most prevalent in closed and patriarchal societies, where males are dominant.

Increasingly, Muslims in the United States are changing these norms. For example, although men and women still stand in their own groups during prayer, it is more common to find both genders in the same room—the women's group praying behind or alongside the men's group. More American mosques are arranging their prayer halls in the side-by-side format so that women can

Women pray silently at the Islamic Center of Southern California in Los Angeles. In many Islamic cultures throughout the world, men and women are segregated in public activities, including group prayer. Increasingly, however, that practice is changing in Muslim communities in the United States.

have equal access to the imam or the speaker. These changes have not gone over well with many Muslims, particularly those who have emigrated from countries with more traditional, patriarchal cultures. In those countries, gender roles and views on the place of women differ dramatically from the norms that prevail in American culture.

The Islamic view of women is one of the most hotly debated topics among Muslims, with individuals from various cultures expressing a range of opinions. Some feel that women belong in the home as wives and mothers; others argue that in addition to motherhood, women should be free to pursue careers.

More Muslim women are joining the debate on gender issues. Those born and raised in the United States—who tend to be especially vocal—often argue (as do Muslim women elsewhere) that throughout Islamic history, male-dominated cultures have used Islam to justify oppressive treatment of women because men, not women, were interpreting the Qur'an and Islamic law. In reality, these women say, the Qur'an and Islam explicitly gave women many rights uncommon in patriarchal societies, including rights of inheritance and property ownership. And the Prophet himself always treated his wives and other women with respect. During his lifetime, women attended the mosque, participated in government and politics, and spoke out in public forums. As role models, Muslim women in the United States today often point to Khadija, Muhammad's first wife, the first convert to Islam; Aisha, his second wife, who was politically active; Sumaiyya, the first person to die for Islam; and Nusayba, who went out to the battlefield to nurse soldiers and protect the Prophet's life. Finally, to those who challenge the right of women to participate in society, they cite examples of countless Muslim women throughout history who were scholars, leaders, and philanthropists.

In order for Islam to be successful in the United States, many American Muslims believe, Muslim women must enjoy the opportunities available to other women in the society: the chance to obtain higher education, pursue a professional career, and even hold public office. And women, they say, must actively participate in Muslim community affairs.

Even when American Muslim women agree on general goals, however, they frequently differ in their approaches. One of the most visible signs of differing approaches is in dress. Islam requires that both men and women wear modest clothing while in public, but interpretations of what constitutes modest clothing vary. Muslim women of certain cultural backgrounds veil their faces and wear long overcoats that cover the entire body except for the hands. Other Muslim women wear the *hijab*, a headscarf. Whereas some Muslim societies, such as Saudi Arabia and Iran, dictate what a woman must wear while in public, in the United States, Muslim women—like all women—are free to dress as they choose. Some cover their entire body, but a greater number simply cover their hair with the *hijab*. Still others cover neither their hair nor their body but prefer to dress in a manner more typical of women in American culture.

American Muslims who wear the *hijab* argue that it has several important benefits. Not only does it identify the wearer as a Muslim, but, supporters say, people interact differently with a woman who is covered. Instead of focusing on her body, they are more likely to focus on her mind, and physical appearance is less

Although the Qur'an enjoins Muslims to dress modestly when in public, it does not specify precisely what should be worn. For Muslim women in some traditional cultures, appropriate attire includes clothing that covers the entire body, including the face. In the United States, many Muslim women simply wear a headscarf called the *hijab*, while many others do not believe it is necessary even to cover their hair.

likely to determine social interactions. On the other side, Muslim women who don't wear the *hijab* believe that it actually attracts more attention to a woman's body because it is not the norm in American culture. They also argue that they can be just as modest and spiritual without covering their hair.

MARRIAGE

In the Islamic tradition, marriage is considered a sacred act. In fact, a well-known hadith says that marriage is one-half of a person's religion.

Marrying and raising a good, faithful family is a priority of Muslim life. The challenge of forming a relationship filled with justice, tranquility, and love is in itself deemed an act of worship. Sexuality, along with marriage, is also regarded as sacred. Islamic tradition does not view it solely as a means for procre-

Family plays a central role in the lives of members of the Nation of Islam, as it does for all Muslims. Pictured here is a scene from the Million Family March of 2000.

ation. Rather, Islam views sex as a necessary and healthy aspect of marriage in which both men and women are entitled to fulfillment. In fact, intimacy between individuals who are married to each other is regarded as an act of worship. On the other hand, sexual intimacy between unmarried individuals is forbidden and considered a serious sin. Also discouraged are situations that might lead to inappropriate physical contact. For example, Islamic law prohibits unmarried men and women from being alone together in a secluded place or engaging in intimate behavior, which includes embracing or holding hands. Not surprisingly, norms of courtship in American society are at odds with these traditional Islamic practices.

Islamic tradition teaches that the most virtuous people are those who choose spouses based on their piety, but it also acknowledges that people often select marriage partners based on other motivations. In many of the world's Islamic countries, the norm is for people to marry within their own racial, ethnic, social, and economic group. (In some places arranged marriages—by which parents choose their child's spouse, often based on such criteria—are still common in rural areas.)

In the multicultural United States, however, young Muslims are much more likely to choose marriage partners from different backgrounds. Like other young Americans, many simply don't see race or ethnicity as a determining factor in marriage. Citing the universal nature of Islam, young Muslim Arabs, Indians, Caucasians, and African Americans are intermarrying in larger numbers. Islamic law also permits Muslim men to marry Christian or Jewish women.

Three main elements are required for an Islamic marriage to take place: an offer and an acceptance, a written contract, and two witnesses. Before the marriage ceremony, a contract is prepared with a written agreement between the man and woman. As a part of the contract, the man is required to pay the woman a dowry—a sum of money that goes directly to the bride and that she can use in any way she chooses. In the early days of Islam, when women had very little social and economic power, the dowry was insurance in the event the couple divorced. Today, however, the dowry is often symbolic—for example, a small sum of money, a beautiful copy of the Qur'an, or a prayer rug. Islamic marriage contracts focus on protecting the rights of women, and many women also include prenuptial agreements in their contract guaranteeing them additional rights, including the right to finish their education, pursue careers, have household help, or have the freedom to visit their family as often as they desire. Two people are required to verify the contract and witness the offer and the acceptance.

Muslims do not have to get married in a mosque; ceremonies may take place anywhere. In a typical ceremony, an imam (or any individual licensed to conduct a marriage) begins with a short sermon about the virtues, responsibilities, and spirituality of marriage. Then he asks the groom and bride or their representatives if they agree under the conditions of the contract to be married. After both have agreed and signed the contract, they are greeted and embraced by friends and family. Later, according to cultural traditions, Muslims hold elaborate receptions to celebrate the occasion.

Even though Islam allows divorce, the prophet Muhammad considered it a last resort, and most Muslims in the world today frown upon the practice. Divorced individuals are often stigmatized and find it difficult to remarry.

GROWING UP MUSLIM AND AMERICAN

How do you raise your children as Americans and still have them maintain their Muslim identity? This is a question that American Muslim parents confront every day. Parents of young children promote Islamic identity and pride through various means. Some take their children to weekend schools. Others try to make sure their children have Muslim playmates. In recent years Muslim-owned companies have provided parents with another tool: videos and programs that reinforce Islamic ideas and give young children a sense of involvement with their religion.

But religious involvement and instruction during childhood provide no guarantee of a strong Muslim identity during the teenage years. Adolescence is a difficult time for Americans of all backgrounds, and Muslims are no exception. In some ways, the issues Muslim teens face are especially difficult. Even more so than their peers, Muslim teens tend to be pulled in different directions by their schoolmates, their communities, and their parents. Parents and the larger Muslim community expect them to stay true to Islamic values and ideals. But this means not socializing with the opposite sex—not dating, and not going to parties, dances, or proms. Because these activities typically make up a significant part

Students at the Islamic Institute of Knowledge in Dearborn recite a Ramadan prayer. In certain respects, Islam and popular American culture pull Muslim children in different directions, and many Muslim parents choose to send their children to Islamic schools in an effort to ensure they will remain true to their faith.

of the lives of other American adolescents, Muslim teens may find themselves constantly standing apart from their non-Muslim peers.

To provide opportunities for teens to socialize with one another and forge friendships in an environment that does not conflict with Islamic values, many Muslim communities have established youth groups. In general, boys and girls are separated within these groups, but when they do interact it is in a religious setting and with close supervision. In addition to purely social activities, youth groups provide young Muslims with moral support through discussions of the difficulties they face in practicing their faith, including such issues as peer pressure, drugs, dating, and sex. Local youth groups also get Muslim teens involved in community service through soup kitchens, meals for the homeless, visits to local retirement facilities, and so on.

The Muslim Youth of North America (MYNA), a national youth organization, sponsors camps and conferences. At these retreats, young Muslims have ample opportunity to socialize, learn more about their religion, and network with other young Muslims from across the United States and Canada. Many attendees have formed lasting friendships with people they met at these camps and conferences, and many couples credit MYNA and other youth activities with helping them meet their future spouse.

As a result of their involvement with Muslim youth groups such as MYNA, many young Muslims develop very strong identities. Girls especially are inspired to wear the *hijab*. And all of the young people are encouraged to be more vocal at school and to participate in community service. A major focus of MYNA and other groups when they first began was to train young Muslims to be community leaders. However, as many of the youth graduated and went to college, they felt that these groups overemphasized leadership at the expense of religious education and spiritual training. MYNA is currently undergoing a transformation in hopes of focusing more on community youth groups and religious education.

MUSLIM ORGANIZATIONS

The Federation of Islamic Organizations, the first national Muslim association in the United States, was formed in the 1950s. Its founders hoped to connect Muslim communities from around the country, but the organization worked along ethnic lines and stressed cultural identity.

The Muslim Students Association (MSA), founded in 1963 by immigrant students, attempted to unify Muslims of all backgrounds.

The Islamic Society of North America, headquartered in Plainfield, Illinois, is the largest mainstream Muslim organization in the United States and Canada. Among other goals, it seeks to support Muslim communities and to promote good relations with members of other religious faiths.

It was based on models from India, Pakistan, and Egypt. More than 40 years later, the MSA remains active on college campuses, addressing the specific needs and concerns of Muslim students.

As the original founders of the MSA settled into American life and joined American professions, they formed a new organization, called the Islamic Society of North America (ISNA). Currently, this is the largest mainstream Muslim organization in the United States and Canada. It sponsors a number of Muslim groups, including the MSA; professional guilds and organizations; and MYNA, its youth chapter. While ISNA has a diverse membership, organizations like the Islamic Circle of North America and the Muslim Arab Youth Association cater, respectively, to the cultural and linguistic needs of Indo-Pakistanis and Arabs. Each of these large organizations sponsors national conferences and publishes a magazine.

Other Muslim organizations have a more political focus. The Council on American Islamic Relations (CAIR) is an advocacy group that monitors government policies toward, and media reporting of, Islamic issues. CAIR has played a key role in identifying, and alerting the Muslim community to, civil rights issues arising in the wake of the September 11, 2001, terrorist attacks. The Washington, D.C.–based American Muslim Council lobbies government officials on international and domestic issues of concern to the Muslim community. The California-based Muslim Public Affairs Council has a similar mission.

In addition to these, Muslims have joined to form many professional organizations and guilds for physicians, lawyers, and artists. There are even several organizations that center on women's issues, including the North American Council for Muslim Women and KARAMAH: Muslim Women Lawyers for Human Rights.

While many of the existing Muslim organizations focus on leadership training, community building, networking, and professional interests, there is a growing realization among American Muslims that there has been a lack of focus on scholarly and spiritual institutions. Consequently, along with a rise in the number of Sufi groups, Muslims have established many new organizations that specifically focus on religious knowledge and spiritual training. Even some of the older organizations are restructuring in order to emphasize spiritual and educational goals. Groups like the Muslim Youth of North America have realized that while it is essential to train Muslims to be good leaders and activists, it is equally or more important to provide them with spiritual education, inspiration, and guidance.

Sunnis and Shiites typically worship at separate mosques in larger U.S. cities. In smaller communities, however, it is not uncommon for Muslims from both sects to share a mosque—one of the unique challenges facing the Islamic community in the United States.

8

Challenges Facing American Muslims

"If thy Lord had willed," a well-known verse of the Qur'an reads, "He would have made humankind into a single nation, but they will not cease to be diverse." Diversity has been a hallmark of the Islamic world, and especially of the Muslim community in the United States. One of Islam's strengths is that it attracts believers from a variety of cultural traditions, and the Qur'an and Islamic law naturally invite a range of interpretations. But diversity also poses challenges, and that is especially true for American Muslims.

Relationships Among Muslims

Muslims are the first to celebrate the vast cultural and ethnic traditions represented in their community. They take great pride in the delectable foods, colorful clothes, and festive traditions that converge in the American Muslim landscape. However, celebrating differences and promoting diversity are two separate issues. Despite the opportunity for Muslims to form a truly universal Muslim community as described in the Qur'an, a small percentage of people still organize themselves around ethnic and racial ties. As more immigrants come from the Arab countries, India, Pakistan, and Southeast Asia, and as more Americans convert to Islam, they find it easier to practice Islam with others of their own background. In large cities like San Francisco, Chicago, and New York, it is common to find mosques whose membership is drawn from a single ethnic group, such as the Arabs, Pakistanis, Afghanis, or African Americans. Seven percent of American mosques have membership from a single ethnicity. These communities provide a place for people with common languages, cultural traditions, backgrounds, and Islamic ideas to socialize and to worship. They remove the challenge of having to deal with other Muslims who may have different opinions and approaches. Disappointed by this trend, most Muslims continue to organize communities where everyone is welcome. All Muslims can interact at mosque and center events in these mixed communities. But, when it comes time to socialize, they often break into their own cultural groups.

African Americans, Arabs, and Indo-Pakistanis are the three largest Muslim communities in the United States. They tend to form very distinct social and cultural groups within the larger Muslim population. Separation is due partly to the fact that each group has its own experience and culture. Because it is natural for people to socialize with others who have common experiences, most Muslims don't see this as a problem. The trouble is that each group interprets Islam differently and feels that its interpretation is the correct one.

Another challenge that faces Muslims is racism. Naively, many Muslims assume that because they are a diverse people, their communities do not suffer from ethnic and racial prejudice. The problem of racism in the Muslim community is unspoken. It comes up in subtle ways—when a Pakistani boy wants to marry a Palestinian girl, when a Syrian boy wants to marry an Indian girl, or when a white woman wants to marry an African American man. As new circumstances arise that call for closer interaction with other races and ethnicities, Muslims often uncover their own racial prejudices. Through intermarriage and friendships, young Muslims are forcing their parents to deal with racial and ethnic issues.

MUSLIMS AND NON-MUSLIMS

"O humankind," reads another verse from the Qur'an, "God has created you from male and female and made you in diverse nations and tribes so that you may come to know each other. Verily, the most honored of you in the sight of God is he who is the most righteous." The Qur'an teaches Muslims to be tolerant with one another and also with people of other faiths. Yet how Muslims relate to other Americans is an issue that has become especially important in the last few years. Many people have accused Muslims of being intolerant of others. In reality, most American Muslims are broad-minded and civil when it comes to their non-Muslim neighbors. They live, work, and socialize with them on a daily basis. Nonetheless, there are those within the Muslim community who are intolerant of others, Muslim and non-Muslim. Believing that their brand of Islam is the only acceptable way of life, they constantly demean, criticize, and even condemn those who do not conform to their ideas.

As the world witnessed on September 11, 2001, such intolerance can have devastating effects. To explain the intolerance, some Muslims have said that the radical Muslims are not a part of the Muslim community or that they are Muslims who are behaving in a manner contrary to the teachings of Islam. However, a growing number of Muslims realize that in order to make changes, they have to accept responsibility for the views of their own community members, no matter how fanatical they are. Faced with this sort of extremism in their own community, Muslims have been compelled to reexamine their own interactions with one another and with their non-Muslim neighbors. More important, they have been rediscovering what the Qur'an and the tradition of the Prophet teach about tolerance. Islamic history, since the time of Muhammad, is filled with examples of religious tolerance. Jews and Christians lived peacefully in many Islamic lands and were allowed to maintain their own traditions and laws. Though the Qur'an encourages Muslims to spread the message of Islam, it also gives great importance to mercy, justice, tolerance, and peace. In order to make a positive impact on society, the Qur'an encourages Muslims to "enjoin the good" and to stand up, at any cost,

The mission of Dar al Islam, in northern New Mexico, is to strengthen Muslim communities in the United States and to build bridges between Muslims and non-Muslims through education. Here students browse in Dar al Islam's library.

for justice. Slowly, Muslims are striving to effect positive changes within their own communities—pushing them to reclaim the tolerant spirit of Islam that is emphasized in the Qur'an and demonstrated by Muhammad in his lifetime.

While they attempt to reform their own communities, Muslims are also trying to build bridges with their neighbors. Islamic organizations and mosques are sponsoring interfaith dialogues. Forums like this emphasize the similarities between American faiths. Dialogues between the three Abrahamic faiths focus on common roots, common approaches, and common social and moral ideas. Local mosques increasingly allow visitors to observe special occasions like Friday prayer and invite guests to participate in Ramadan activities.

IDEOLOGICAL COMMUNITIES

Muslims come to live in the United States for many different reasons, including education, economic opportunities, and the freedom to practice their faith without interference from the government. Among Muslims in the United States, commitment to the Islamic faith varies, as does involvement in U.S. society.

As with other faith traditions, Islam has its share of nonpracticing members. In the United States, nonreligious Muslims tend to assimilate; for them religion is often seen as an aspect of their cultural identity that no longer has much importance.

Other Muslims choose to fully integrate Islam into their daily lives. Many of these Muslims have devoted considerable resources to contributing to Islamic organizations and building up their religious communities in the United States. They have invested large amounts of time and money to establish institutions, schools, and mosques.

At the same time, many of these devout Muslims also view the United States as their home. Some, of course, are American born. But others who immigrated have found that the United States offers opportunities that were unavailable to them in their coun-

Pakistani Americans show their support for the United States during a
march in Brooklyn following the terrorist attacks of September 11, 2001.
American Muslim leaders condemned the attacks as contrary to the tenets
of Islam.

tries of birth. Many even say they have experienced a degree of
religious freedom unavailable in many Islamic countries. Many
admit that they left countries with dictatorial governments that
were particularly oppressive toward intellectual Muslims. In the
United States, these individuals have the opportunity to excel in
their fields and to practice Islam in a way that is not constrained
by government policies. Thus, for many, getting involved with
American life is a priority. As active members of American society, they make contributions, they vote, and they participate on
school boards and city committees, hoping to make life better for
all Americans.

A large number of Muslims in the United States feel that their
purpose in this country is to make *da'wa*, to propagate the message of Islam. According to them, it is not acceptable simply to

make a good impression and to generate understanding among non-Muslims. In their view, Muslims should actively spread their faith and encourage people to convert. Like many Christian missionary movements, they distribute literature and engage in debates and dialogues with people of other faiths. They especially focus on minority groups like the African American and Hispanic communities. Members of this ideological community go to great lengths to distinguish themselves from the rest of American society. Because they view themselves not as an integrated part, but more as visitors with a message, they maintain very cultural forms of clothing and appearances.

After World War II, many Muslims came to the United States seeking educational opportunities. Arabs, Indians, and Pakistanis,

In the view of some Muslims in the United States, merely fostering good relations with members of other faiths is insufficient. Like certain Christian missionaries, they believe it the duty of devout Muslims to win converts.

who were already well educated in English and Western culture, often remained and joined the professional workforce. They became doctors, engineers, and professors and were the ones who began serious community-building efforts.

Muslim students continue to come to American colleges and universities from abroad. As they are in the United States on student visas, they return home upon completion of their studies. For the most part, they bring a wealth of knowledge and experience to the Muslim community. However, some, knowing that their stay is temporary, tend not to get involved with American life. Many even come from countries that have negative views toward the United States, and many maintain their negative sentiments about American government and popular culture even as they study in American schools. Entrenched in their cultural practices of Islam, they are often critical of American Muslims, whom they see as having sold out or as practicing a watered-down version of the religion. Frequently they come from countries that have a highly standardized, strict interpretation of Islam, or countries where governments interpret Islam and use it to maintain the status quo. Unable to adjust to the diversity of American Muslims, they often feel the need to impose their own views, which leave very little room for differences based on experience, environment, or culture. American Muslims, especially the young, are often deeply affected by these strict interpretations of Islam brought by Muslims from other countries. The lack of a strong American Islamic scholarship, as well as the not yet fully developed Islamic culture, have left American Muslims unsure of who they are and how and where they belong. Many even question their role as Americans. Looking for a sense of identity and belonging, some adopt clothing and traditions typical of other Islamic countries. Muslim women who already wear scarves sometimes adopt even more conservative forms of dress such as face veils and overcoats. In search of a spiritual and cultural identity and frustrated with the inadequate educational and spiritual opportunities available in the United States, many young Muslims have started to go abroad, to study Arabic and Islam and to live in Islamic countries for short periods of time.

AMERICAN MUSLIMS AND THE WORLDWIDE MUSLIM COMMUNITY

Many American Muslims strongly identify with fellow Muslims all over the world. They are deeply affected by events in Islamic countries, especially tragedies and wars. Using their rights as American citizens, many have pressured the U.S. government to aid suffering Muslims or to take political action where Muslims are being oppressed. Perhaps the greatest source of Muslim disappointment with the United States is the American stance on the Israeli-Palestinian conflict. In the view of many Muslims, U.S. policy is one-sidedly supportive of Israel and often overlooks Israeli human rights violations against Palestinians. However, countless Muslim rallies, political organizations, and lobbies have been unable to affect the government's approach to the issue.

LIFE AFTER SEPTEMBER 11

September 11, 2001, was a terrible tragedy for all Americans. Three thousand lives were lost on that day. Gone, too, was the nation's sense of security.

American Muslim leaders and Islamic organizations quickly condemned the attacks—which had been perpetrated by 19 Arab Muslim extremists who had come to the United States primarily on student or tourist visas. President Bush also urged Americans to differentiate between peaceful, devout Muslims and the Muslim terrorists. Nevertheless, some Americans viewed all the Muslims in their midst with suspicion, and a few lashed out violently. Anti-Muslim hate crimes—including attacks on mosques and assaults on people wearing traditional Muslim clothes—spiked. Only 28 such incidents were reported in 2000, according to the FBI, but in

Some Muslims have equated America's "war on terrorism" with a war on Islam.

2001 that number jumped to 481. Some Muslims, fearing violence, did not leave their homes for weeks after September 11.

If the short-term effect of September 11 on many Muslim Americans was to undermine their sense of safety and belonging in U.S. society, the long-term effect, some critics charge, may be even more dire. New anti-terrorism laws enacted in the wake of the attacks threaten to erode the civil rights of Muslims, these critics charge. One law, for example, required men from predominantly Islamic countries to register with the government and be fingerprinted. In addition, many Muslims were detained for months by the government, without being charged and without having access to an attorney. A large number of these people had been picked up for minor violations of their immigration status; many were eventually deported.

The attack on the World Trade Center was a wakeup call for American Muslims. Since the tragic events of that day, they have had to seriously reevaluate their communities. Many wonder how Muslims could commit such heinous crimes in the name of a religion that is so focused on beauty, tolerance, and peace. As one American Muslim scholar puts it, "Such groups ignore the history of the Islamic civilization, with all its richness and diversity, and reduce Islam to a single dynamic—the dynamic of power. . . . In the world constructed by these groups, there is no Islam; there is only opposition to the West."

In the aftermath of the al-Qaeda-sponsored terrorist attacks, many American Muslims have turned their focus inward, striving to improve their understanding and practice of Islam. Here: A believer inside a Washington, D.C., mosque.

The Future of Islam in the United States

Eager to reclaim the true beauty of their faith, many American Muslims are starting to focus inward—on themselves, on their communities, and on American society at large. Islamic activism is starting to take a new shape. Whereas a decade ago Muslims were perhaps more intent on spreading the message of Islam and on speaking out on international causes, now they are focused on improving their own understanding of their religious tradition. Practicing Muslims are refocusing on the basics of Islam—praying, fasting, and giving charity. Personal development, character training, and a renewed interest in the great Islamic tradition are a priority over activism, especially among young Muslims. According to many Muslims, this is the only way that they can ensure that they don't misrepresent or do injustice to the teachings of Islam. A popular American Muslim leader claimed that on September 11, Islam was also "hijacked." But many Muslims are realizing that they unwittingly supported the trends that removed spirituality and beauty from Islam and reduced it to a political tool.

FOCUSING ON THE COMMUNITY

Mainstream Muslims are also paying closer attention to their communities. In addition to strengthening national institutions, they are also focusing on community development. Especially after September 11, Muslims are aware of the need for Muslims to unite and to support one another. They are renewing efforts to integrate Muslims of all ethnicities and backgrounds. At the same time, more communities are also supporting efforts to educate others about Islam—not necessarily because they want people to convert, but particularly to correct misconceptions and misunderstandings about Islam. Mosques and community centers are increasingly open to interfaith activities. They have also started outreach programs that work with schools, churches, and synagogues to promote a healthy relationship between Muslims and their neighbors.

Though Muslims are still advocating the causes of their fellow Muslims worldwide, they are also increasingly addressing Muslim issues within the United States. Recent threats to their civil rights have compelled them to become more vocal on American issues. Many believe that once they establish a stronger presence in the American political arena, they will be able to effect more change in American foreign policy toward Islamic nations. In addition to international issues, Muslims are asserting their views about policies that affect American society. As they become more engaged in local and state politics, Muslims are advancing issues such as schools, the environment, the criminal justice system, and national safety.

In order for Islam to thrive in the United States, according to American Muslim scholars, Muslims need to contribute to American life. Islam, they argue, encourages them to effect change and to contribute to humanity at large. By developing charitable endowments and social services, they can demonstrate their commitment to improving the United States. Additionally, young Muslims must continue to enter new fields so that Muslim communities can have access to social workers, counselors, attorneys, and legislators who can truly address their issues and speak on their behalf.

To ensure a bright and secure future, the greatest necessity and challenge for Muslims may be to establish their own scholarship in the United States. Because American Muslims have their own unique problems, strengths, issues, and challenges, they need Muslim jurists and theologians who know the United States as well as they know Islam. American Muslims can no longer rely on the guidance of foreign shaykhs and scholars who have never lived in the United States and know very little of American life. Furthermore, they cannot rely on non-Muslim scholars and commentators to tell them what their problems are and how to solve them, how to strengthen their communities, or how to practice Islam in America. American Muslims must figure this out for themselves. To devout Muslims, this is a true jihad—a true inner struggle. As the Muslims grow in number and interact with others, and as they find their way, the quality of their culture, their impact, and their future will be determined by how honestly they struggle and how true they stay to the spirit of Islam.

Chronology

ca. 1875   First wave of Muslim immigration to the United States begins.

1913   Noble Drew Ali founds the Moorish Science Temple of America.

1918   The beginning of the second major wave of Muslim immigrants.

1930   W. D. Fard founds the Nation of Islam.

1934   Fard disappears, and Elijah Muhammad becomes the Nation of Islam's leader; the first new mosque constructed in the United States is built in Cedar Rapids, Iowa.

1947–60   Upsurge of Muslim immigration from the Indian Subcontinent and Eastern Europe.

1963   The Muslim Student Association (MSA) is formed at the University of Illinois.

1964   Malcolm X leaves the Nation of Islam, makes the pilgrimage to Mecca, and converts to mainstream, orthodox Islam.

1965   Expansion of Muslim immigration follows the repeal of national-origin immigration quotas.

1968   Islamic Circle of North America (ICNA) is begun.

1975   Wallace Muhammad becomes the leader of the Nation of Islam when Elijah Muhammad dies.

1980   Wallace Muhammad changes his name to Warith Deen Mohammed.

1985   Warith Deen Mohammed dissolves the leadership structure of his group so that his followers can become orthodox Sunni Muslims.

1981   Islamic Society of North America (ISNA) is founded.

1990   Warith Deen Mohammed opens U.S. Senate with prayer, becoming the first Muslim to do so; American Muslim Council is established in Washington, D.C.

Chronology

1994 Council on American Islamic Relations is established in Washington, D.C.

1996 A mosque is incorporated into the Denver International Airport. The Pentagon hosts a Ramadan meal for Muslims.

2001 Islamic extremists hijack four passenger jets, crash two into the World Trade Center in New York and one into the Pentagon near Washington, D.C.; the fourth plane goes down in a field in western Pennsylvania. In the aftermath of the attacks, hate crimes directed at Muslim Americans rise, and legislation is enacted that, critics charge, infringes on the civil rights of Muslims.

2003 A coalition led by the United States invades Iraq during what American president George W. Bush calls a "war on terrorism," removing Iraqi head of state Saddam Hussein from office. Responses from Iraqi Muslim-Americans are mixed.

2004 Reports of abuse of Iraqi prisoners by American soldiers at Abu Ghraib prison are made public, accompanied by graphic photographs. President Bush condemns the incidents on Arab television stations.

2005 The Fiqh Council, a group of Muslim-American scholars of Islamic law, issues a fatwa against religious extremism and terrorism; over 100 other Muslim-American groups endorse the statement.

2006 Many European Muslim groups protest depictions of the prophet Muhammed in political cartoons appearing in a Danish newspaper; American media is torn on whether to display images of the cartoons when reporting the story.

Glossary

adhan—call to prayer given at the time of each of the five daily prayers.

Allah—the Arabic word for God.

dhikr—remembrance of God.

Hadith—the sayings and deeds of the prophet Muhammad as reported by those who witnessed them.

hajj—the fifth pillar of Islam; a pilgrimage to Mecca, which all Muslims who are able are supposed to make at least once in their lifetime.

halal—permissible to eat according to Islamic law.

hijab—a head-covering worn by some Muslim women.

imam—in the Sunni tradition, a religious leader who leads the prayer; in the Shiite tradition, a descendant of Muhammad who is the divinely chosen leader of the community.

iman—the second level of Muslim spiritual understanding, during which belief is internalized.

ihsan—the third and most profound level of Muslim spiritual understanding.

hijra—the migration of Muslims from Mecca to Yathrib, which was renamed Medina, in 622.

jihad—inner struggle against the unwholesome part of one's nature; struggle against oppression and the enemies of Islam.

Kaaba—a temple in Mecca that, according to Islamic tradition, was built by Adam and rebuilt by the prophet Abraham and his son Ishmael.

mosque—A Muslim place of worship.

Glossary

salat—Islamic ritual of prayer; performed at least five times daily and on other special occasions.

sawm—fasting during the daylight hours in the month of Ramadan.

shahada—the first pillar of Islam, a declaration of faith.

Sharia—Islamic law.

Shia—one of the two major sects of Islam; members of this sect are called Shiites.

Sufism—a mystical tradition that emphasizes the inner aspect of spirituality through meditation and remembrance of God.

Sunna—the traditions of the prophet Muhammad as exemplified by his actions and words.

Sunni—the largest sect of Islam.

Tawhid—the unity of God, the most fundamental principle of Islamic faith and worship.

umma—the worldwide community of Muslims.

wudu'—ritual washing and purification before performing *salat*.

zakat—required alms payment or charity.

Further Reading

Abou El Fadl, Khaled. *The Place of Tolerance in Islam*. Boston: Beacon Press, 2002.

Curtis, Edward E., IV. *Islam in Black America.* Albany: State University of New York Press, 2002.

Nasr, Seyyed Hossein. *Islam: Religion, History, and Civilization*. San Francisco: Harper San Francisco, 2003.

Nyang, Sulayman S. *Islam in the United States of America*. Chicago: ABC International Group, 1999.

Smith, Jane I. *Islam in America*. New York: Columbia University Press, 1999.

Turner, Richard Brent. Islam in the African-American Experience. Bloomington: Indiana University Press, 1997.

Wolf, Michael, ed. *Taking Back Islam: American Muslims Reclaim Their Faith*. Emmaus, Pa.: Rodale, 2002.

Wormser, Richard. *American Islam: Growing up Muslim in America*. New York: Walker and Co., 1994.

Internet Resources

http://www.cair-net.org

The Council on American Islamic Relations is a Muslim advocacy organization that keeps track of Muslim civil rights and provides information to the public on American Muslim concerns.

http://www.islamicity.com

A resource on various aspects of Islam, Muslims, and Muslim life in the United States. Topics range from the Qur'an to advice from imams to politics and media.

http://www.isna.net

The home page of the Islamic Society of North America provides information and news regarding Muslims in the United States.

http://usinfo.state.gov/products/pubs/muslimlife/homepage.htm

The U.S. State Department provides information about Muslim life in the United States, including population demographics, family life, and education.

http://www.masnet.org/

The home page of the Muslim American Society.

Bibliography

Abou El Fadl, Khaled. *The Place of Tolerance in Islam*. Boston: Beacon Press, 2002.

Anway, Carol L. *Daughters of Another Path: Experiences of American Women Choosing Islam,* Lee's Summit, Mo.: Yawna Publications, 1995.

Austin, Allan D., ed. *African Muslims in Antebellum America: Transatlantic Stories and Spiritual Struggles.* New York: Routledge, 1997.

Barboza, Steven. *American Jihad: Islam After Malcolm X.* New York: Doubleday, 1994.

Chittick, William C., and Sachiko Murata. *The Vision of Islam*. St. Paul: Paragon House, 1994.

Curtis, Edward E., IV. *Islam in Black America*. Albany: State University of New York Press, 2002.

Diouf, Sylviane. *Servants of Allah: African Muslims Enslaved in the Americas.* New York: New York University Press, 1998.

Haddad, Yvonne Yazbeck, ed. *The Muslims of America*. New York: Oxford University Press, 1991.

Haddad, Yvonne Yazbeck, ed. *Muslims in the West: From Sojourners to Citizens*. New York: Oxford University Press, 2002.

Haddad, Yvonne Yazbeck, and Adair T. Lummis. *Islamic Values in the United States: A Comparative Study*. New York: Oxford University Press,1987.

Haddad, Yvonne Yazbeck, and Jane Idleman Smith. *Mission to America: Five Islamic Sectarian Communities in North America.* Gainesville: University Press of Florida, 1993.

Haddad, Yvonne Yazbeck, and Jane Idleman Smith, eds. *Muslim Communities in North America,* Albany: State University of New York Press, 1994.

Bibliography

Haddad, Yvonne Yazbeck, and John L. Esposito, eds. *Muslims on the Americanization Path?* Atlanta: Scholars Press, 1998.

Haley, Alex. *The Autobiography of Malcolm X.* New York: Ballantine Books, 1964.

Haque, Amber. *Muslims and Islamization in North America: Problems and Prospects.* Beltsville, Md.: Amana Publications, 1999.

Hasan, Asma Gull. *American Muslims: The New Generation*. New York: Continuum, 2002.

Kennedy, Brent, and Robyn Vaughn Kennedy. *The Melungeons: The Resurrection of a Proud People: An Untold Story of Ethnic Cleansing in America*. Macon, Ga.: Mercer University Press, 1997.

Koszegi, Michael A., and J. Gordon Melton, eds. *Islam in North America: A Sourcebook*. New York: Garland Publishers, 1992.

Leonard, Karen Isaksen. *Muslims in the U.S.: The State of Research.* New York: Russel Sage Foundation, 2003.

Lin, Phylis Lan, ed. *Islam in America: Images and Challenges.* Indianapolis: University of Indianapolis Press, 1998.

Metcalf, Barbra Daly, ed. *Making Muslim Space in North America and Europe.* Berkeley: University of California Press, 1996.

Muhammad, Amir Nashid Ali. *Muslims in America: Seven Centuries of History*. Beltsville: Amana Publications, 1998.

Muhammad, Elijah. *Message to the Blackman in America*. New York: Secretarius Publishers, 1997.

Mohammed, Warith Deen. *Focus on Al-Islam*. Chicago: Zakat Publications, 1998.

Mustafa, Ayesha K., ed. *Focus on Al-Islam: Interviews with Imam W. Deen*

Bibliography

Mohammed. Chicago: Zakat Publications, 1988.

Nasr, Seyyed Hossein. *Islam: Religion, History, and Civilization*. San Francisco: Harper San Francisco, 2003.

Nimer, Mohamed. *The North American Muslim Resource Guide: Muslim Community Life in the United States and Canada*. New York: Routledge, 2002.

Nyang, Sulayman S. *Islam in the United States of America.* Chicago: ABC International Group, 1999.

Smith, Jane I. *Islam in America*. New York: Columbia University Press, 1999.

Turner, Richard Brent. *Islam in the African-American Experience*. Bloomington: Indiana University Press, 1997.

Waugh, Earl H:, Sharon M. Abu-Laban; and Regula B. Qureshi, eds. *Muslim Families in North America.* Edmonton, Alberta: The University of Alberta Press, 1991.

Wolf, Michael, ed. *Taking Back Islam: American Muslims Reclaim Their Faith.* Emmaus, Pa.: Rodale, 2002.

Wormser, Richard. *American Islam: Growing up Muslim in America.* New York: Walker and Co., 1994.

Index

Numbers in **bold italic** refer to captions.

Index

Index

Index

Picture Credits

Contributors

General Editor DR. KHALED ABOU EL FADL is one of the leading authorities in Islamic law in the United States and Europe. He is currently a visiting professor at Yale Law School as well as Professor of Law at the University of California, Los Angeles (UCLA). He serves on the Board of Directors of Human Rights Watch, and regularly works with various human rights organizations, such as the Lawyer's Committee for Human Rights and Amnesty International. He often serves as an expert witness in international litigation involving Middle Eastern law, and in cases involving terrorism, national security, immigration law, and political asylum claims.

Dr. Abou El Fadl's books include *The Place of Tolerance in Islam* (2002); *Conference of the Books: The Search for Beauty in Islam* (2001); *Rebellion in Islamic Law* (2001); *Speaking in God's Name: Islamic Law, Authority, and Women* (2001); and *And God Knows the Soldiers: The Authoritative and Authoritarian in Islamic Discourse* (second edition, revised and expanded, 2001).

Dr. Abou El Fadl was trained in Islamic legal sciences in Egypt, Kuwait, and the United States. After receiving his bachelor's degree from Yale University and law degree from the University of Pennsylvania, he clerked for Arizona Supreme Court Justice J. Moeller. While in graduate school at Princeton University, where he earned a Ph.D. in Islamic Law, he practiced immigration and investment law in the United States and the Middle East. Before joining the UCLA faculty in 1998, he taught at the University of Texas at Austin, Yale Law School, and Princeton University.

General Editor DR. SHAMS INATI is Professor of Islamic Studies at Villanova University. She is a specialist in Islamic philosophy and theology and has published widely in the field. Her publications include *Remarks and Admonitions, Part One: Logic* (1984), *Our Philosophy* (1987), *Ibn Sina and Mysticism* (1996), *The Second Republic of Lebanon* (1999), *The Problem of Evil: Ibn Sina's Theodicy* (2000), and *Iraq: Its History, People, and Politics* (2003). She has also written a large number of articles that have appeared in books, journals, and encyclopedias.

Dr. Inati has been the recipient of a number of awards and honors, including an Andrew Mellon Fellowship, an Endowment for the Humanities grant, a U.S. Department of Defense grant, and a Fulbright grant. For further information about her work, see www.homepage.villanova.edu/shams.inati.

ANJUM MIR is a teacher, journalist, artist, and mother of two who lives in the Los Angeles area.